Building Plans For Poultrymen

And Practical Methods of Poultry Raising

by H.V. Tormohlen

with an introduction by Jackson Chambers

Self Reliance Books

Get more historic titles on animal and stock breeding, gardening and old fashioned skills by visiting us at:

http://selfreliancebooks.blogspot.com/

Introduction

I am pleased to present yet another title on Poultry.

This volume is entitled "Building Plans For Poultrymen" and was published in 1920.

The work is in the Public Domain and is re-printed here in accordance with Federal Laws.

As with all reprinted books of this age that are intended to perfectly reproduce the original edition, considerable pains and effort had to be undertaken to correct fading and sometimes outright damage to existing proofs of this title. At times, this task is quite monumental, requiring an almost total "rebuilding" of some pages from digital proofs of multiple copies. Despite this, imperfections still sometimes exist in the final proof and may detract from the visual appearance of the text.

I hope you enjoy reading this book as much as I enjoyed making it available to readers again.

Jackson Chambers

Kellerstrass Farm

Arthur Oscar Schilling
1907

1

Starting Right in the Poultry Business.

Each year finds many new recruits in the poultry industry. The poultry journal solicitor with his aggressive friendly way meets you at the county fair or poultry show and asks you point blank, "Do you raise chickens?" You admit that you were raised on the farm and although you do not happen to be so fortunate as to be raising fowls now you certainly have a "feeling" that way. Accordingly you subscribe for the journal on the strength that it will tell you all about how to raise poultry.

But many of the poultry journals have too much of the professional air about them and the person starting with fowls finds himself in deep water as far as understanding what a great many articles are about. Too many of us forget the time we got our first setting of eggs and just how eagerly we read every word we could find on how to rear chicks, feed, make coops and all the varied problems of poultry keeping.

I did, like many of you have just done, answered an advertisement of one of the breeders claiming to have 57 varieties of land and water fowls. We got the immense catalog and then could hardly sleep nights thinking what an immense farm that breeder must have and if we only had it we would be in paradise, as far as this world is concerned. Somehow we are all after something cheap and at bargain prices. These little one inch ads scattered about in the periodicals and strangely quite scarce in the poultry journals have an enticing way about them.

The beginner who subscribes for a good poultry journal and commences to get in touch with the breeders advertising in them is on the right track. The poultry journals carry advertising for a livelihood and do not be afraid, Mr. Beginner, to place your order for stock or eggs with any of them for the poultry journal cannot afford to keep scoundrel advertisers more than a month. Therefore you are protected and you need have no hesitancy in placing your order with breeders who are making a life study and specialty out of their variety. These are the breeders to tie to. They are giving their individual attention to their variety and are anxious to help you get started right. Do not be taken in by ads found in the cheap magazines and farm papers. You may get value received and you may not.

Decide upon the variety you like best and then go at it in earnest. Do not make the mistake of trying out a half-dozen varieties to see which is best. You will know little more about it at the end of a year or two than you know now. Decide upon one of the well advertised varieties for there is certainly merit in a variety that is widely advertised. Decide whether you want to breed for meat or eggs. Also whether for fancy or utility or a combination of both. Make up your mind for all time to come to stick to it. Making a success with poultry is principally sticking to it and profiting by your own experience. If you want to breed for meat choose one of the larger varieties. If your tastes run to lots of eggs take up one of the lighter egg breeds for they will produce more eggs as a rule and on less feed per egg than any of the heavier varieties.

The next thing to decide is how much you can afford to put into getting stock or eggs this first season. Make up your mind you are going in to win financially and as to quality of your stock. Therefore do not be misled into getting cheap stock yourself, into believing you will buy cheap stock and then breed up for how can you, a person with no experience in breeding poultry, make much headway in the next five years breeding up your cheap flock to a better flock. Answer the advertisements of breeders advertising stock of the variety you have chosen and ask them frankly what they would advise you as a beginner to do. All of them will tell you that the best is none too good and that the best pays in the end while the beginner who starts with the cheapest stock or eggs he can find with the idea of breeding up, finds after a few years dear experience that he must dispose of all his stock and start all over with stock several grades higher than he has. Too many beginners scan the advertisements for the cheapest stock or eggs they can find offered. The only one I ever knew who made a success at this was a red-headed boy friend of mine who became interested in my thorobreds and decided to embark himself in fowls. He decided upon White Leghorns but had only 50 cents. I loaned him 50 cents until cherry picking time and he found an advertisement of 25 eggs for $1. He hatched 23 chicks and raised 21 of the lot and in the fall sold a trio for $10. That was a pretty good investment. But even this boy saw he must have better quality and to make a success he had to keep this cheap blood out of his flock with the care as if it were a contagious disease for whenever he introduced it into the better fowls he subsequently got, he found he had trouble with quality.

Make it your policy to go slow and get the best. Rather buy one setting of $5 eggs than 100 eggs for $5 for the chicks from the $5 setting eggs will likely be worth more than a dozen raised from the $5 per 100 eggs. Often you can raise 10 or more chicks from a single setting but do not count the money lost if you succeed in saving one chick for nine out of ten chances he will be worth more than you paid for the setting of eggs.

If you have a little back yard you have all taht is necessary. I started with a back yard, without a sign of a fence or coop. I made the mistake of starting with a cheap incubator and brooder. The brooder burned up with all the chicks after the second hatch but I got valuable experience.

Buy a good incubator or brooder or what is better for the beginner hatch your first year or two eggs with hens. Get acquainted with nature's way. You can buy setting hens at this time of the year most anywhere for 50c to $1 each. Get your hen and make a nice nest in an empty barrel in the back yard. Put a few glass eggs under her and darken the front and leave her 24 hours. Order your eggs for you will have little trouble getting the hen to stick to business. Face the barrel to a little run if possible. Keep the hen quiet. Furnish her with plenty of corn and wheat and water and grit. See that she returns to the nest the first few days and by the time the eggs arrive she will be attending to her nest without coaxing. Nothing beats a barrel for setting a hen in. It is roomy and the hen walks into the nest instead of jumping down into the nest and breaking the eggs as so many do when a box is provided. The barrel out on the ground is just near enough mother earth to make an ideal place just as nature would have it should you find the jungle fowl with her nest built in a thicket or underbrush in the wild.

Keep the hen dusted with a good lice powder twice during the period of incubation and a protection of a few boards up in front of the barrel while she is on the nest, especially at night to guard against possible accident thru a cat or dog or rat bothering the nest and you will have splendid success with the eggs. If you want to raise several chicks the first season a good plan is to set two or more hens at one time and then reset one hen. A hen fed and cared for well can easily incubate two clutches of eggs without any harm or cruelty to the hen and the other hen can raise the first lot of chicks. I have had hens weigh more at the end of six weeks than they did at the start simply because I gave them proper feed and care.

Raising Poultry as A Side Line.

To the suburbanite and small town dweller the raising of poultry offers many wholesome, enjoyable hours of outdoor employment during the year if indulged in merely as a side line if fowls are kept only for the purpose of furnishing the table with choice spring fries and broilers and eggs the entire year.

The advantages to the business man in raising poultry in the few feet of back lot or on the half acre at the suburban home are many. There is no employment that offers to the person who is closely confined by office work a greater amount of light physical exercise, or a more pleasant means of recreation than the culture of thorobred poultry in a limited way.

To the person who can interest himself in this industry, and who can devote spare time to it with the idea of gaining not only physical exercise, but of acquiring a knowledge of the business that will enable him to excel as a fancier, there is a fascination about the work that increases as experience is gained. The tilling of the soil for the garden of flowers or vegetables is an enjoyable recreation but the garden plot lasts only for a few weeks at the most and during that time very strenuous work it is indeed, while the rest of the year—at the very time when indoor workers need fresh air most—the garden cultivates habits of cozy fire-side physical idleness. Our friends, the chickens, require attention each and every day of the year and so we are forced to get out and stir up the straw litter in the scratching shed with the thermometer about the zero mark on those cold winter mornings the same as in July. Thus the habit of getting out and exercising in the cold fresh morning air is formed and— good habits if formed in town invariably insures health and happiness.

It is said that a well balanced variety of tasks makes one task a recreation for the other and to come away from the city and office with its cares and intense mental exertion and hurry out to the poultry headquarters and attend to a nice flock of busy but care free hens makes life take on a different aspect and the close association with nature relieves the pessimistic and bewildered mind in a very short time. Poultry raising as an occupation might grow monotonous in a very short time to the office man with a brain trained and accustomed to grasp big problems and solve them but as a diversion from the daily grind and routine of life, poultry raising forms an excellent safety valve for the strenuous brain worker.

Starting in to raise poultry may be done on a very small scale or on a more elaborate scale if much experience in the rearing of poultry has previously been acquired. Starting with a couple of old "biddies" and two dozen chicks is much more satisfactory even to those who have had experience for be it remembered that in this day and age of the world chickens cannot be raised like we used to see our grandmothers back on the farm raise them and even if we know a great deal about it because of being reared on the farm or spending the summers at grandmother's we will encounter difficulties in raising chicks on back lots that we never heard of before.

The different breeds of thorobred poultry today are so far superior to mongrel stock for the different purposes for which they were developed that it is nothing short of folly to raise anything but thorobred stock. Your individual tastes will have much to do in selecting a breed but do not be unduly influenced by the popular opinions of the day. Tomorrow the fad will be over and you will be wanting to change breeds for the new arrival in popular favor which is declared to be the "greatest layer and best broiler ever."

Eggs are practically indispensible in the modern kitchen

and they are used every day in the week while a dressed fowl is used probably once a week. Nice fresh eggs seem to be the hardest to get on the market the year round while seldom, if ever, is a nice carcass hard to procure. For this reason I would deem it the better plan to keep fowls primarily for eggs and secondarily for meat. Then again where the young birds must be continually confined their carcasses when ready to fry, will have cost more for feed than if purchased on the market as the broiler man on the farm can raise and market fowls much cheaper on his acres than the city man can on the back lot where he must purchase every morsel of feed.

But eggs can be produced with about one half the market price of eggs from a good laying strain of hens when confined in very limited city quarters the year thru..

There is no best breed or variety. But there are better strains of layers among the different varieties. One Plymouth Rock will lay better than another because it has come from a long line of ancestors which have been bred for egg production.

Senator Mooney of Mississippi recently asked an old colored man what breed of chickens he considered the best and he replied, "Marsa Mooney, all breeds of chickens has de merits, for instance the white ones am de easiest to find after dark and de black ones am the easiest to hide after you once gits em."

I chose Brown Leghorns because I had known from a small boy up that they were noted layers of white eggs. I had seen some flocks of white birds in town and they always presented a dirty appearance. These were the reasons why I decided on the Brown Leghorns but your way of looking at it might lead you to an entirely different conclusion and you might decide on the Minorcas, the Houdans, the Anconas, or the Rhode Island Reds. Then again as a student of colors as found in nature I found the Brown Leghorns presented the deepest mysteries and difficulties in combining the shades of any of the Gallinaceous tribes. I found it very hard to produce show worthy specimens at first and for several seasons my efforts proved a failure in that at least I was unable to produce as good specimens as the parent stock itself. But after delving in nature's laws I finally worked out the principles as to how to mate to make colors reproduce themselves. Indeed, it was such a fascinating study that every leaf and flower and painting that came under my eye was observed closely for some hidden combination or principal in color combinations.

To start in the spring in raising fowls it would be desirable to purchase baby chicks or eggs from some reliable breeder and place them under a setting hen which you have bargained for from some neighbor who keeps mongrel hens or some farmer friend. Setting hens should be purchased for not over $1.00

apiece and they can be sold for 75 cents when the chicks are raised. The chicks can be kept in a small coop until nearly grown and in the fall a poultry house can be built.

How to Make A Piano Box House.

A great many people who raise poultry, either on a large or a small scale, will find the plans for a cheap poultry house given here are just the thing for which they have been looking. They will appeal especially to the city man who can keep but five or six hens and on rented property possibly, and alike to the large poultry raiser for colony houses to be moved about the farm in the green fields during the summer. There are hundreds of these colony houses in use on the largest poultry farms in the country.

The ease with which the house can be built commends it to those who are not skilled carpenters and who do not have the time to build an elaborate house. The house is modeled on the most approved lines of poultry house construction, being a combination of the open and canvas front types, and having the shelf dropping board under the roost, which is along the back wall to catch all the droppings while the fowls are on the roost during the night. If a small breeding pen is kept in the house the space beneath the dropping board is utilized for nests and the floor, which is covered with several inches of straw, for scratching.

Piano boxes for different makes of pianos differ slightly in size. The ordinary box is from five feet to six feet in height by five or a little over long, the back generally being square. They are two and a half to two and three-quarters feet wide at the bottom.

After getting two piano boxes of the same dimensions we remove the backs and tops shown in the illustration, The backs are then spread out as shown and sawed in the portions inicated by the arrowed lines.

Two piano boxes of the same size, with tops and lids removed, are required for the house.

The one back is sawed into halves while the other is sawed into halves and one of these halves halved again. These quarters form the topmost part of the roof with an additional six or eight inch board.

The second half numbered 3 forms the floor between the two boxes. Half of number four fits in at the back between the two boxes while number five is used for the dropping board. All the additional lumber required for the house are the two by

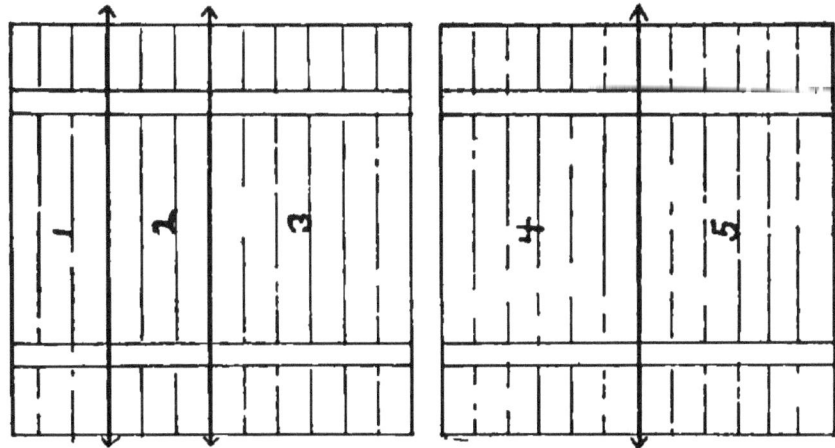

The two backs of the boxes are cut as shown by the arrow lines in above illustration. The method is described in full in accompanying article.

Completed piano box poultry house

fours under the floor and for the roof and one by fours for the door. No glass windows are required for the house as the light is admitted thru the open front door. The door is merely covered with wire netting. During a very cold winter night a canvas curtain is hung over the wire netting and fastened onto buttons on the frame of the door. As the whole house is covered with tarred paper or some good roofing paper it is surprising how comfortable and warm the fowls keep in this style of house and yet with the canvas off the front of the door almost every day in the year. Only about three months of the year need the canvas be used in the central states even at night, as the more fresh air the better after the fowls become accustomed to this mode of housing. The general tone and health of the flock is greatly benefited by the fresh air type of house.

These houses make excellent ones in which to keep an outdoor brooder early in the season and they may be used at every stage of the work of poultry raising.

Some Pitfalls in the Way of a Beginner.

I remember as if it were yesterday my first season's work with poultry—my first real earnest determined effort at being a poultryman, altho I had worked with poultry some each year since a small boy, when as a chap of three I had a pair of bantams given me and with them the first germs Galli which later developed into a bad case of "hen fever." I can remember each difficulty and obstacle which I had to overcome and can still see those mountains which I had to cross altho at the time I was often so discouraged and disheartened that I often thot I would give up. I can therefore appreciate the position of every amateur at the poultry business as I have been all along the road and know the trials and troubles and know just how big some of the obstacles look to you while in a year or two you will look back and have to take a magnifying glass to find them.

Remember the poultry business never was, is not now nor ever will be all peaches and cream, but also remember that the longer you stay in the game the easier it is to play it and of course, the fewer the obstacles, the more enjoyment and profit.

After careful observation I am convinced that infant mortality with new born poultry enthusiasts is just about as great as it is with infants. The chances for quitting the business are in about the same proportions as the death rate in infants, if not greater. Like infants, if the amateur poulterer lives his babyhood of two, three and five years out without deceasing in any respect his enthusiasm and love for the fancy, he can be counted on to live to a ripe old age as a fancier. It is a matter of common knowledge among poultymen that the great majority of people quit the chicken game quite at the end of the first, second, or third year. Therefore, take heart and have courage, you who have newly started raising poultry and look forward to the better days ahead, if you feel it is all one grand round of troubles. If, tho, you are so enthusiastic at this stage of the game to feel like you never would quit and have read this article to this point, read it thru if you care to, but if not, lay it aside carefully where you can turn to it hastily a little later when a "fit of the blues" comes over you.

Taking up some of the common every day troubles of the new beginner, we will take them in their order with the season.

Probably some are having trouble in keeping their parent stock in the pink of condition. To be in good condition and health the fowls must be fed right, housed right and not crowded. If your fowls seem out of condition, give them more park and house room. Give plenty of sunshine and fresh air and water. If you are having trouble in getting fertile eggs or are getting soft shelled eggs, your troubles come under this same general head. Keep a dry mash before your fowls all the time, composed of three parts ground corn, two parts bran, two parts middlings, two parts gluten feed, and one part beef scraps. Keep grit, oyster shell and charcoal before them and with the dry mash, fresh water, dry litter to scratch in, your breeding stock will take on more life, lay better and the eggs be more fertile. If possible, get them out on the grass whenever you can.

If you have trouble in getting the hens to set after changing them from one nest to another, change them after dark after this and have the new nest dark and so the hen can be inclosed in it. Place your eggs under her the second day and watch when she leaves the nest for a week until she becomes accustomed to returning. If laying hens eat eggs, make all nests so dark that the fowls cannot see the eggs after getting in the nest. If the setting hens begin to break eggs, you have built the nest wrong, and she breaks the eggs when she jumps down on the nest when returning. Close the nest on top and have the entrance on the side where the hen can walk right in on the eggs. When you find the eggs smeared up with a broken egg, wash them off in luke warm water, change the nesting and they will be little worse for the wear.

Keep the setting hens free from lice by dusting with lice powder often. Do not grease the setting hen. Feed principally whole corn and wheat to the setting hens with plenty of grit and water and they will hold out in fine flesh.

In operating the incubator, follow the directions carefully. If you have lost the directions, write for more. Keep the lamp clean by wiping carefully after filling each time and you will not notice the oil fumes.

If you have had trouble with the chicks sticking in the shell spread a piece of cheese cloth over the eggs twice a day for the last five days which has been wrung out in warm water.

If the chicks die in the shell get more fresh air to the eggs and keep ventilators wider open during next hatch.

After the hatch, keep the chicks under hen or in incubator first twenty-four or thirty-six hours. This is much more important than feeding them.

After putting them in the brooder be sure to keep them from chilling the first week especially. Chilling means bowel trouble, white diarrhea, lack of life and loss of many.

Leg weakness is caused by warm brooder floors and crowding. If your chicks show general debility they have been overfed or are bothered with lice.

To get best results with small chicks, feed a variety of food. Keep plenty of grit and clean water before them. Also plenty of bran. Then by feeding chick feed in the litter and an occasional feed of stale bread, moistened with milk, hard boiled eggs, lettuce leaves, raw apples, the chicks will lack for nothing and will do well. I have found it a safe rule when the chicks are not doing well on the feed and I am in doubt as to the trouble, to feed a variety.

The chicks should be treated with carbolated vaseline, salty grease or grease with little kerosene added for head lice every two weeks for eight weeks. Head lice kill more chicks than the general poultry public is aware of.

Clean the brooder often. Whitewash all coops in which hens and chicks are kept. Do not try to make one hen do the work of three by giving her thirty chicks to brood. She will make a failure of it until they die off, until only about eighteen or twenty remain, if that many.

Where little chicks pick each others combs and toes and seem to have a craving for blood, get them out in the open and on grass runs and feed milk or beef scraps. Isolate the ones that have been picked so they will not be injured farther and to keep the rest from going farther with the habit.

In case of gapes, a parisitical disease, where the chicks stand around and seem to gasp for breath, moisten the throat with turpentine, use a gape worm extractor, or place chicks in a box and sift some air slaked lime over their heads until they sneeze or gasp for breath and shake their heads violently when the worm will be dislodged and sneezed out.

White diarrhea is a disease of small chicks that has caused many a poultryman to quit the business. Volumes have been written on it. Only the last two or three years have our agricultural colleges found the cause and remedy after it has once gotten a start in the flock. The only word we will give it here is to say that you will never be bothered with it if the parent stock is kept in large runs and fed and cared for properly. If the chicks have it the disease was transmitted thru the egg to the chick. Some have advocated washing the eggs to be incubated in a weak solution of alcohol to free the eggs from the germs. There are several good remedies on the market to combat the disease in the chicks. Home remedies will be of little use. Heroic efforts must be made to save a flock of little chicks after they once have become incubated with the disease. It is a significant fact that brooder chicks are much more susceptible to it than hen brooder chicks.

By all means make it your policy, when starting in with poultry to raise a few well than to raise a whole lot and make a miserable failure before the summer is half over. The great mistake made by all beginners is that they attempt too much. On the average village or city lot, fifteen to thirty chicks is the greatest of plenty. Think of the town dweller on a lot 50x60 getting the "chicken fever" and attempting to raise two hundred chicks to maturity on that small space. It will keep one man busy digging graves during June and July when nature is doing her best to right the trouble by killing off 90 per cent to give the 10 per cent a chance to live..

Among my friends and acquaintances each season I number two or three who have the "chicken fever" and attempt too much and are down and out before the end of the year. Consider yourself fortunate then if you read these lines and profit by them.

I will mention only one of these failures in passing as they are all similar except in setting. My young friend, newly married, came to me for advice about raising chickens on his back lot. Thought it would be profitable recreation and furnish the family table with fresh eggs and broilers. Wanted a thorobred, as he wanted to have a nice looking flock and birds that he could show. The first season he raised thirty-five on the back lot. Fine success, hardly a one dying, due to the fact that the lot had not had chickens on it for some time. By fall he had become so infatuated with his flock that he wanted to keep the majority over for breeders, having visions of a great poultry farm by this time and must save every one of these to make the nucleus for the start of his poultry farm. I tried to dissuade him from such a hasty move when he came to me for advice, but he insisted that he was tired of town life and was planning on leading the back-to-nature life and in a year or eighteen months at the most would be on the farm. Asked for poultry house plans, but after reading a description of the two best, had an idea of his own and built one according to his own idea which would beat any yet. Before the winter was over a great number of his fowls had the roup in this house, which was away too small by this time for the growing youngsters. In the spring bought a ten dollar prize winning cockerel, a fine strong fellow. Only got three chicks out of seven settings of eggs, set under hens, and not a chick out of 100 eggs in the incubator, all caused by the lack of vitality and crowding of hens. Cockerel proved all right on other hens. Before the end of the second summer he wanted to sell me his $40 house for $20 and his fowls for a song, as he was greatly disgusted with the "chicken business," and his whole trouble was in attempting too much, overcrowding, and failure to pay any attention to advice and warning of those who had raised fowls for years. Many of the trying obstacles that confront the novice may be obliterated by putting into practice the teaching of this article.

Essential Requirements of A Poultry House.

From Pennsylvania State College Circular No. 39.

The essential requirements of a poultry house are comfort for the hens and convenience for the attendant. It should be economical in construction, cheerful, well ventilated and sanitary.

Location—In choosing a location for a poultry house, the following factors should be considered:

(a) A southern or southeastern exposure is best because it insures the largest amount of sunlight during cold weather. The house will be more cheerful and the fowls will get out earlier in the spring.

(b) Shelter. While sunlight is essential, the poultry building should be sheltered from the intense heat of the sun during the hot months and from the full force of prevailing winds. If possible, use of natural shelter such as trees, an orchard, a hill, or a barn.

(c) Water Drainage. The poultry house must be dry. Select a location that provides natural water drainage.

(d) Air Drainage. Air drainage is as important as water drainage. Avoid a location that allows cold, damp air to settle around the poultry building.

(e) Convenience. Locate the poultry house in as convenient a place as is consistent with the requirements of exposure, shelter and drainage. The poultry building should be easily reached from the house and other farm buildings.

Portable or Permanent House. A portable colony house should always be used for chicks and growing stock. It may also be advantageously used for housing the breeding stock. When a large flock is kept for egg production a large permanent house will be most economical. Unless two large yards can be provided for the permanent house, the portable colony houses will give better results. Poultry should not be kept in the same location more than two years in succession.

Size. An 8x12 ft. colony will comfortably house 25 fowls. Equipped with four portable hovers or a colony brooder heater, it will care for 150 to 200 chicks from the time thru the eggs are hatched until maturity. For laying hens, four squ the eggs to or space should be provided for each fowl. For egg production, hens may be profitably housed in flocks of 100 to 500.

Yards. The close yarding of fowls in long, narrow yards is to be avoided as much as possible. Small yards are difficult to till, increase the cost of equipment, increase the labor of caring for the fowls, and tend to make the latter restless and discontented. Give the fowls the free range of a large field. Let them run in the orchard, pasture or corn field. If yards must be used, provide a double yarding system. One yard can be tilled and sown to grass or clover for pasture while the fowls occupy the other. This is necessary in order to avoid disease and to provide an economical supply of green food.

Type of House. Some form of fresh air house should be used for poultry of all ages. Poultry will thrive in rather cold houses if they are dry and provide an abundant supply of fresh air without drafts. Fresh air is of more importance than warmth.

Floor. The essentials of a good floor are a hard surface, smooth enough to be easily cleaned, dryness, durability, economy construction and warmth. It should be rat proof. A common cause of dampness in a poultry house is a poor floor.

The three most common floors are earthen, board and cement.

Earthen or Dirt Floor. Altho it has a low initial cost, it is liable to be damp and hard to clean. It harbors mice and rats and must be replaced every year. The final cost is high because of labor required to keep it clean.

Board Floor. This is best for a portable house; it is sanitary, fairly inexpensive, durable and may be made rat proof by lining underneath with fine mesh wire.

Cement Floor. This is the best for a permanent house, as it is rat proof, easily cleaned and very durable. It is liable to be cold, however, and is more expensive than other types.

Walls. The walls should provide warmth, dryness and strength for the house. They should be cheap, durable and easy to clean and disinfect. They should be high enough in front to admit sunlight to the back part of house. A height of 4½ to 5 feet is sufficient for the rear wall. The front wall should be 6 to 8 feet in height depending upon depth of house and type of roof. Double walls are not necessary. Walls should be tight on all sides except the front. Rough boards covered with roofing paper and grooved siding or flooring may be used.

Roof. The types of roof most commonly used are the shed, gable, combination and "A" roofs. The "A" roof is adapted to small colony brooder houses. The shed roof may be used on houses not over 15 feet in depth. The gable roof is adapted to small colony houses for breeding stock. For large houses over 15 feet in depth, use the combination or double pitch roof.

Roofing Materials. Prepared roofing materials are most

satisfactory. Shingles require a 1-3 inch pitch and are expensive. Tar paper is not durable. Use a good grade of roofing.

Windows. All windows, both for light and ventilation, should be placed in the front of the house. Both glass and cloth windows should be used.

Glass windows should be long and narrow, placed vertically and high up. This allows the sun the fullest sweep over the floor with the least amount of glass area. Use 8x10 inch, or 9x12 inch glass. Provide one square foot of glass for each 12 to 15 feet of floor space.

Cloth windows are used for ventilation. They should be rectangular in shape, placed horizontally, and high enough to protect the fowls from wind and storm. Provide one square foot of cloth surface for each 10 or 12 feet of floor space. Use a good grade of unbleached muslin. The cloth window should be kept open as much as possible. Close it only on very cold nights, during a storm, or on dark, damp, cloudy mornings.

The cloth windows should be hinged at the top to swing in and up.

The combined cloth and glass surface should be approximately one-third of the area of the front side.

Doors. These should be of convenient size, wide enough to permit a cart or wheelbarrow to enter. Outside doors should swing in.

Alley Way. An alley way is not advisable. It occupies valuable floor space, is expensive both as to construction and labor, increases the air space in proportion to the number of fowls that may be cared for, thus making the house cold, and it prevents intimate contact with the flock.

Interior Fixtures. These should be portable to make cleaning easier and to aid in controlling lice and mites. They should be as few in number and as simple in design as possible and should be so placed that fowls may have the range of the entire floor.

Plans for Poultry Houses. So many conditions must be considered in building poultry houses that each individual must, in the end, plan his own house.

The Right Soil for Poultry Yards.

When the place for the poultry quarters is selected, generally little attention is given to the character of the soil, although this is one of the leading factors in being successful in the raising of poultry.

When poultry is raised as an adjunct to the average American farm fowls are generally given the liberty of the farm, be it clay, sandy, muck, or loam, level or rolling ground, and from hence forward they are left to shift for themselves. The hens are allowed to roost in some abandoned shed, in the trees or a poultry house is built on a spot of ground which could not possibly have been used for any other purpose. The house has one or two small windows with a generous portion of the panes broken out and the whole house is built with the sole idea of it being a roosting place and not to be used during the day, as the roosts are built after that well known stairway style of architecture, with the first roost near the floor and to the front, and one rising above the other, until the last is well up under the roof. The fowls roosting upon the topmost roost show their supremacy, as this is the choicest place and cannot be easily reached by the good wife wishing a hen to fill the pot for the Sunday dinner, or when company unexpectedly comes. With this state of affairs it is a matter of the survival of the fittest. The fowls shift about for themselves for their food and they take their choice of scratching in the chaff in the barn, roaming about in the pasture, field or orchard or wading about in the shallow water of the creek or ditch in quest of morsels of food. All the Gallinaceous tribes have wonderful faculty of adaptability when given their freedom, as they will roam about and find the place most suited to their liking and welfare, and remain there the greater part of the day, only returning to shelter at night, but the moment the attempt is made to confine them to a certain limited territory then the quality of the earth upon which it is intended they are to be placed must be taken into consideration as well as providing them with a house to be used during the day as well as night.

The kind of soil best adapted to poultry raising is rolling, shady or gravelly soil. Fowls thrive better on this kind of soil and need less attention than they do any other kind. The reason is obvious. Where fowls are kept in any great numbers the ground upon which they tramp day after day quite naturally becomes filthy. The sand and gravel soil, being looser and lighter, the surface does not become so compact and the fowls keep the soil stirred up to certain extent with their scratching. Then, after each rain this soil is fresh again as the water becomes dirt-laden and quickly soaks away.

With a clay soil, even when rolling, or hilly, quite to the contrary is the rule, as well as with a muck soil. The more a clay soil is tramped the more compact it becomes, added to its naturally very compact state. Then when poultry offals and rain are added, instead of the filthy water running off or soaking up quickly, it tends to stand upon the surface and gradually dry up, leaving a coating of germ-laden filth upon the ground, which is constantly being added to and in a short time fit for neither fowl nor beast to live on until it has been plowed or spaded. When it is taken into consideration that filthy and unsanitary quarters are the source of nearly all the evils in the poultry yard, then the importance of a naturally healthy footing for the fowls may be realized.

With a heavy soil the only safe way to keep the poultry healthy, and the soil clean as well, is by frequently turning the soil and sowing it to some forage crop whenever possible. A high and dry place, even with sandy soil, should be chosen for the poultry runs and houses where there is an abundance of drainage. Then the runs should be ample and two runs for each pen of fowls. Each alternate run then can be turned under and sown to a mixture of lettuce, rape, oats, and wheat, and whatever the fowls relish and thrives well in the locality during the summer. Just as often as one run becomes divested of its crop of green the fowls are turned into the other one which has been growing a crop in the meantime. One run then is being sweetened up by the growing crop, while the other is used by the flock, and vice versa. Then late in the fall one run should be sown to rye, which furnishes an excellent late winter and spring green crop. By this method of alternating most any soil, high enough to prevent surface water from standing on it, will yield good returns in the keeping of fowls when handled in an intelligent manner and housed in light, airy houses with clean floors and scratching sheds with plenty of litter to keep the hens busy. In exceptional cases in towns and cities, where a few hens are kept in very limited quarters and the runs are overshadowed so by buildings that it is impossible to grow green foods successfully in the runs to keep them sweet and sanitary, the runs should be covered with several inches of coarse coal cinders and a little soft earth spread over. This surface will keep clean better than almost anything else used for poultry runs.

Why Some Succeed and Others Fail.

If we analyze the characters of the successful and the unsuccessful poultry keepers, we will find an explanation for the quantity and quality of poultry raised by each set of people. One is satisfied with the grade of poultry he now raises, and if he saw a way open for betterment he would lack in determination to have better; while on the other hand the other class reads or is told of better stock and other poultry keepers' methods that are superior to theirs, and by "determination" they go into their work of improving what they already have. Can we afford to say that all those who are not successful in reaching what they desire are lacking in determination? I think not, because we find men who are striving for better, but for the lack of proper training fail. Then we can say that for the lack of determination or training or both, they make failures.

The word "experience" rules success and failure more or less, and the best way of getting it is to be determined that whatever you want to learn will be accomplished one day or another.

While determination and experience are very vital and of so much importance, yet, unless one has proper stock to begin with, houses to protect them in, suitable quarters for them to exercise in and wholesome, practical food to grow on and produce whatever is expected, he cannot expect very much in return for his labors. I am satisfied that there are thousands of "cull" hens, "roosting in tree tops" and getting their "food wherever they chance to find it" today. Still the consuming populace is wondering why eggs and poultry meats are so high. Where you find one farmer getting eggs from his hens during the cold winter days, you will at the same time find two that get none at all. Every neighborhood has its intelligent and "I'll go" people in it; those who are aware that if you expect to get something out of anything you must first put something into it. Again, there are those who realize this fact, yet for the lack of "I will" fail to make any headway in life.

It requires grit, gumption and go to be a successful poultry raiser, and unless you are blessed with these you had better take up some other calling in the business world, for poultry culture is one of the most businesslike vocations to be found. Poultry culture is one line of business which needs men who have and use business "go" and methods.

Still another drawback with many who fail is the lack of proper selection in the breed that is kept and the best stock that is raised each year for future breeding purposes. There are thousands of the best pullets that find their way to market because they developed faster, while at the same time thousands will be kept at home for future breeders, because the huckster wouldn't take them on acount of undersize.

You will not find men entering any kind of business unless they are somewhat familiar with its general working principles yet we find those who will buy a large farm, stock it to its full capacity and begin raising chickens without any previous experience. No wonder, when we consider some methods used, that so many lose out on their poultry ventures. The only reason for it, too, is that the hen side of farm work has always fallen to women and children, until people had decided that any old way would do. At the present stage of advancement one must be qualified, having much of "I'll go" and the proper kind of material to run his poultry venture on, to be anywhere near a successful poultryman.

A Model Poultry House at Reasonable Cost.

Poultry house architecture has gone thru as many and radical changes and has progressed quite as much in the last few years as dwelling house architecture. Only a few years ago the poultry house was merely a roosting room, and was dark and poorly ventilated. Then to make a success with the flock it was found that the poultry house should be made a living room for the fowls, during the winter months at least. It was then that the glass front house sprang into prominence. Whole south sides of houses were made of glass. But these houses absorbed so much heat during the day and cooled off so rapidly in the evening that the health of the fowls soon became seriously undermined. With this style of house, too, the problem of

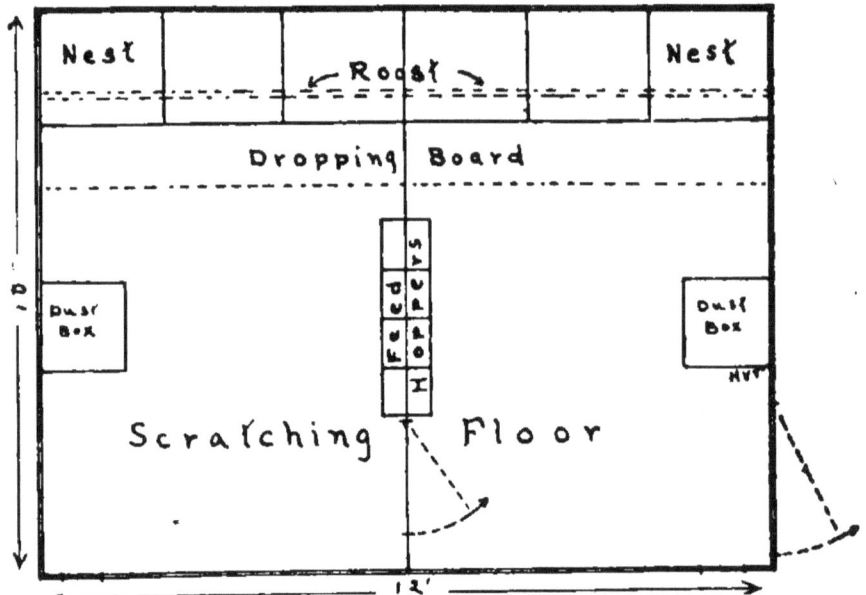

proper ventilation never became satisfactorily solved. Popular opinion then went to the other extreme and we had poultry houses with canvas fronts and now we have them with the front entirely opened. The difficulty with the canvas front was the lack of sunshine which the fowls so much crave during the cold winter months. The canvas front admitted fresh air in abundance but obstructed the direct rays of the sun. The open front house admitted both, of course, but these houses do not protect the flock from the severe and many changes of the weather enough to make the getting of eggs every month in the winter a certainty.

Primarily, all poultry houses should face the south or south-east, and the one door should invariably be on the east end. The ground upon which the house is built should be well drained and with a sandy or gravel surface if possible. Near or in an orchard makes an ideal place.

The design of the house shown is pleasing architecturally and combines economy and convenience. Built as planned with cement floor the combination canvas and glass front, a warm, dry and sanitary house is assured. These, together with an abundance of sunshine and fresh air, are the prime requisites of a good poultry house.

A trench for the foundation is dug one foot wide and one foot deep. Coarse grout cement is filled in the trench and the

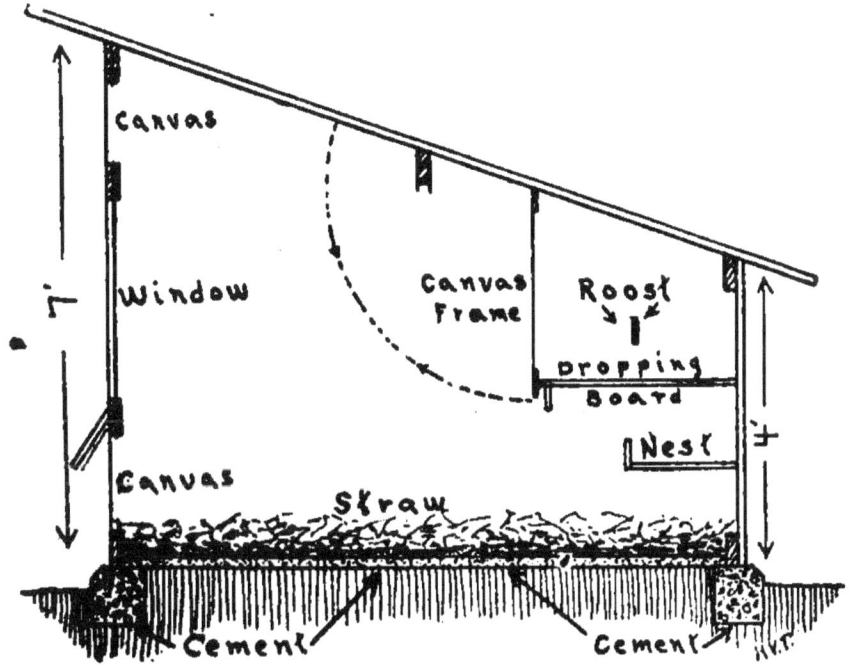

foundation is built six or eight inches above the surface. The part of the foundation above the surface is made of a greater proportion of cement. The earth dug out of the trenches is filled in under the floor. Coarse stone, gravel or cinders is used to fill in the floor within an inch of the top of the foundation. This should be tamped down very tight. A thin layer of coarse cement—an inch to an inch and a half in thickness in sufficient for poultry house flooring—is filled in on the cinders. Finish the floor out with an inch of richer concrete for a top dressing. This need not be blocked out or smoothed as painstakingly as concrete sidewalks. It will be noted that the two by fours and siding nailed to them are dropped an inch or more below the surface of the floor made by imbedding a two by four in the cement above the foundation and removing it after the cement hardens. Dropping the siding thus below the surface of the floor prevents water from beating rains flowing in under the siding and upon the floor as it does quite frequently where the house is built upon a flat surface cement floor.

The house may be made from tongue and grooved siding or cheap rough lumber and covered with roofing paper. In either case the roof should be covered with cheap sheathing lumber and with a good grade of roofing paper or felt. Shingles or tin should not be used in any case. The sheathing should be laid in the roof across the short dimension of the roof by the interior elevation, to eliminate many rafters, and to make the roof tighter upon the framework.

Below is approximately what is required in the way of lumber, for the building:

Seven 2x4's 12 feet long. Three 2x4's 8 feet long. Three 2x4's 4 feet long. Four hundred square feet of lumber for three sides and the roof.

The house is ten by twelve feet, the roof twelve by fourteen and the house seven feet high in front and four in the rear. Do not make the mistake of making a larger house. This house will accommodate twenty-five hens easily and if a larger flock is kept several of these houses should be built about the orchard. Fowls will not do so well where they are kept in large houses or large flocks. It is more natural for six or ten fowls to roam about together. The house is divided into two parts or pens thus making the work of caring for the fowls easier and giving each bird a better chance. The partition dividing the pens should be built up solid about two feet high, so the fowls cannot fight thru the cracks. Above this may be wire netting.

A single roost or perch is made along the north wall well up under the roof. It should be placed about fifteen inches from the roof and the same distance from the rear wall. A shelf dropping board thirty inches wide is built six or eight inches beneath the roost. This should be made of flooring or hard pine and painted with pitch to make it impregnable to moisture. With a rake or hoe the board may be cleaned in a moment of time. Three or four nests in each part are built directly beneath the dropping board. The dust boxes are also built up off the floor about twelve inches thus leaving the entire floor space for the straw litter for scratching. The floor should be covered with six or eight inches of straw at all times into which the small grains are thrown which furnishes the fowls exercise, so beneficial to their health.

A canvas curtain tacked upon a frame is hung in front of the roost to drop down and meet the front edge of the dropping

A cheap and practical poultry house. A house suitable for twenty-five hens and one that can be built at a nominal cost. Its strong points are simplicity of construction, beauty and practicability.

board. It is used only on very cold nights. With this curtain down the fowls are enclosed in a cozy little compartment with plenty of fresh air passing thru the canvas all the time.

The windows, four in number, may be 24 inches by 24 inches or 20 by 30 inches. They are placed midway between the top and bottom of the house. The space above and below the windows is covered with canvas which may be tacked to the two by fours or on frames and hinged to the two by fours so they may be opened during the summer. The windows are made to take out so the house may be left as open as possible during the summer. Frames of one inch wire netting are desirable to protect the windows on the inside and to be used during the summer while the window frames are removed. With the two trap doors at either corner of the house no other opening should be made in the house except the large door in the east end. The north, east and west walls should be made wind tight and the roof fitting down perfectly tight upon these three walls. This house then will be draft proof.

It will be noticed that a board one foot wide projects over the lower canvas and the eave extends out at least twelve inches at the top, so that cold, beating rains may not soak the canvas and then freeze, thus retarding the ventilation. The wide eave not only protects the front, but, as it extends all around the house, it also protects the walls and keeps the ground immediately around the house from becoming so thoroughly water-soaked during wet weather. Carbon-dioxide gas, the principal ingredient of the expired breath of an animal, is heavier than air, and damp air, it is also known, sinks to the floor and thus the reason for the canvas below the window and near the floor. Warm air rises and the house becomes quite warm during the sunshiny days even in winter if there is not a way of ventilating the upper portion of the house and so the reason for the canvas above. No system of trap door ventilator or drafts has been found practical in poultry house ventilation. They either do not ventilate at all or cause drafts. The canvas permits a constant diffusion of air without drafts. With the canvas frame down in front of the fowls at night the air must pass thru two sets of canvas. If the roof fits down tight and there are no cracks admitting air about the walls of the house this combination of glass and canvas front will make as cheap, convenient, attractive and serviceable house as can be built and combs will not freeze until the temperature drops many degrees below zero.

A Poultry House That is Different.

Herewith is presented the plans and description of a poultry house that is built radically different from most of the accepted plans. The idea for this house was suggested by A. V. Thompson, Salt Lake City, Utah, and is used with success by him.

The house fronts south and may be built from any convenient lumber that is at hand as most of it is protected by the roofing paper or material. The width is six feet, the height six and three-quarters feet, and the length twelve feet.

The bottom of the house is made box fashion of one inch stuff and is two feet high. The back is boarded up tight and if practical, is covered with tarred paper the same as the roof. It is hardly necessary to cover the sides with the roofing paper as the eaves extend out over them and protect them from wind and rain alike. The roof is six feet from the drip to the cone. A window is placed in the roof on the east side well to the front and is covered with wire netting from the inside and a door or lid to fit down tight from the outside when the weather is very bad or it is raining. There need not be any glass for this window for whenever it is nice enough for the sun to shine in it is nice enough to have it shine directly in without being obstructed by the glass. A small ridge or raised place must be made under the roofing paper all along the roof just above the window so the rain cannot seep down under the lid when closed.

Above the two feet base in front and to the roof it is covered with muslin as shown in the illustration. Another door should be provided beside the muslin or canvas as shown in the illustration and covered with one inch wire net-

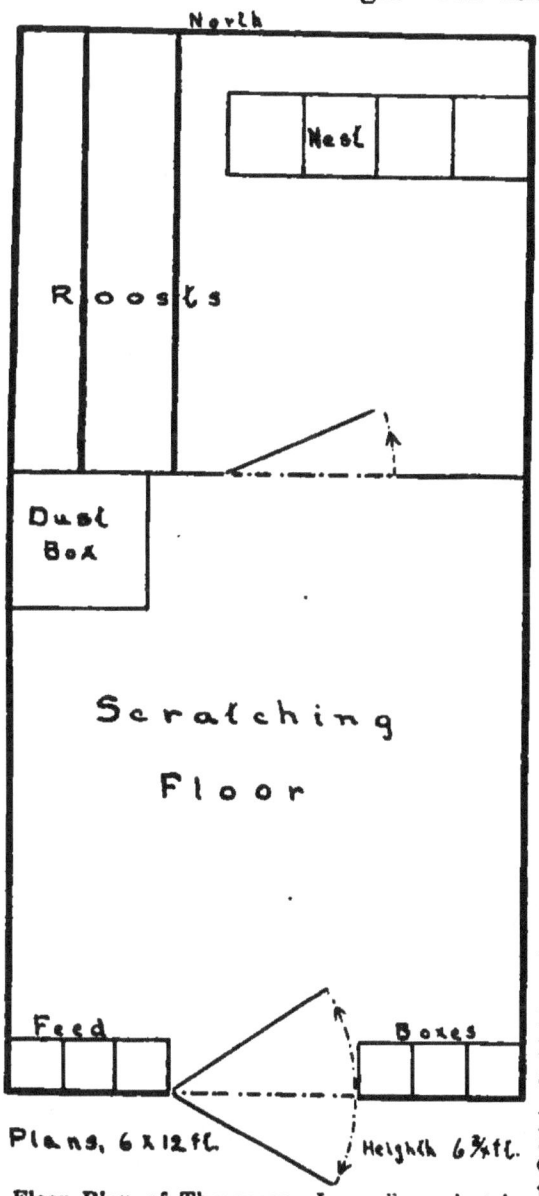

Floor Plan of Thompson House Described by Mr. Tormohlen in Accompanying Article.

ting. The one door can swing out and the other in. Most of the time the inner door, only, will be used.

The ground plan of this house is interesting in that it is quite different than most houses now advocated. Mr. Thompson saye he does not like dropping boards as they are too much trouble and he does not like the nest under the dropping board as they are too hard to get at and to keep the lice and mites out of, so he places the roosts in a second compartment in the back of the house down under the roof on the west side and the nests he places up off the ground as indicated and with the entrance for the hens at the rear. Of course, then, it is so dark in this nest that the hens never learn the egg eating

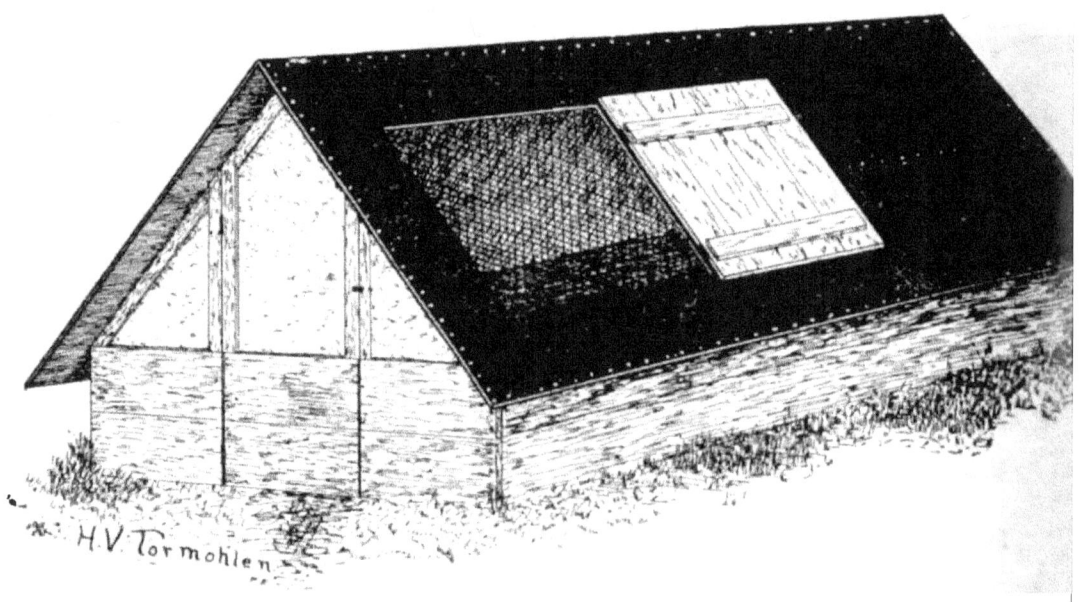

H. V. Tormohlen

habit nor do they fight over the nest. A little trap door or lid is made in the back of the nest from which the attendant can remove the eggs. This is quite handy. Straw to the depth of six inches is placed under the roosts to catch the droppings and this is removed whenever necessary and clean straw put in. It is strange how men's experiences differ with poultry. For my part I think the dropping board one of the modern conveniences and nothing could be easier for me to clean and to go back to the old fashioned way with no dropping board would almost cause me to lose my chicken experience altogether, but this is where man's ideas differ about what is work and what is play.

A muslin partition is placed between the roosting room and scratching floor and during the coldest nights the door to this part is closed. As a rule though it is left open. With this door closed the roosting room of this house would be one of the warmest that could be imagined. With the same thought, I think this house would be most too hot with all the windows and doors out during the summer for poultry to roost in comfortably. This house would rather be for the extreme northern fancier and those on the plains where high winds are prevalent as it is economical from a use of lumber standpoint and is so low that it could be kept warm where most houses could not.

Six foot fanciers, like myself, would not take readily to this house, I am afraid, for to be practical, a house must be high enough to permit the attendant to stand erect in all the working space in the house. This is the principal draw back to these plans.

Mr. Thompson fills the whole house with about six inches of wet clay or earth and tamps it down tightly for a floor. The scratching room floor is covered generously with straw and into this he feeds all the grains. The feed boxes or hoppers are filled with charcoal, grit, oyster shell, beef scraps and bran and chop. This house will accommodate twelve birds easily.

A Practical Small House for Fowls.

Some of the poultry keepers think that the coop or house in which they keep their fowls is one of the least important things connected with the work. This is where many people make their first mistake which results in failure. Proper housing of the fowls should come first in our consideration. One should never purchase chickens unless he has a proper place in which to keep them. The coop illustrated in connection with this article is to my mind an ideal one, both for the large and small fancier. It answers all requirements for all seasons of the year. It can be located at any convenient place, but the window should face the south. Almost any kind of lumber is suitable for constructing the coop. The one important feature is that the coop must be tight and dry. In case the boards do not fit closely together, the sides of the house can be covered with a good roofing or tar paper. The same material can be used for the roofing. It will be noted by referring to the sketch that the entire coop is under one roof, but it is divided into two appartments. For the purpose of describing the construction of the house we will call the left half of it section A and the right half section B.

The sides of the entire coop are boarded tightly with the exception of the door and opening in section A and the door, window and ventilator in section B. The two sections are separated by a partition which has but two openings, the door and the exit for the fowls. Section B has a board floor while section A has a ground floor. The former is raised about six inches from the ground to prevent damp. The window should be made as large as possible as light is essential. There should be an opening in section A covered with a small mesh wire and on the outside of this a curtain or canvas to pull down in the winter time. The interior of section B should be the same as any other coop. The nests should be about eighteen inches from the floor, the dropping boards under the roosts and the curtain

The left half of the house is referred to as section A and the right half as section

in front of the roosts which may be pulled down during cold weather. Section A should contain litter about six inches deep. Section B is the sleeping quarters of the fowls and section A is the scratching compartment which serves as a refuge for the fowls in cold and rainy weather when it is not advisable to allow them to run out into the yards. I believe that this house is really without faults and I am sure that all who try it will be pleased with it. I have not specified the size because the house can be built large or small according to one's needs.

Back Yard Poultry House.

Poultry house construction is without a doubt the most important factor in poultry management. Without a suitable poultry house it is impossible to obtain the most profit from the poultry flock. Disease and vermin are hard to control. The vitality is apt to be lowered and even with the most efficient ration, good results cannot be hoped for. For these reasons, the first step after securing the right kind of stock is to provide suitable homes for the poultry flock.

On the opposite page is illustrated a type of house that is very practical and of the right size for the average family flock, as it will conveniently house from twenty to twenty-five birds.

Among the first things taken into consideration with this design, or these working drawings, are cheapness and simplicity in construction. It will be noted that the only two-by-fours required here are three six-foot pieces on which the floor is laid, the walls being nailed to cleats of same thickness as the boards forming these different sections.

The largest boards shown are the roof and floor boards, which are eight feet, but should boards of this length not be available, they could be laid the narrow way of the coop, which, of course, would make them six feet long. However, if the latter is done, it will be necessary to lay the two-by-fours lengthwise of the coop, which would increase them two feet in length.

The longest boards required for the walls are five feet, running down to three feet in length, which will enable us to use such old lumber as may be lying around the yard, or using the boards from old shipping cases, etc.

Nests should be about eighteen inches square, two on each side, under dropping board. The bottom of the nests are to slide on cleats to which the boards of the side wall are nailed, and the top of nests to be guided with a cleat nailed to bottom of dropping board. This method you will find very convenient in gathering the eggs, which should be done several times a day in freezing weather.

As for the sash, it will be noted that no glass sizes are marked, as it is quite possible that second hand sash may be purchased, which might vary a little from sizes shown.

Under certain conditions, I would suggest covering the entire outside of coop with water proof building paper to eliminate any draught through the cracks, but this is a matter to be considered according to the climatical conditions.

The hopper and drinking fountain should be kept off the floor for the purpose of keeping them clean when the fowls scratch in the litter for their feed.

The scratching shed is to have no floor, as the fowls enjoy dusting themselves in the dirt, which is an excellent remedy or preventative for lice and mites.

The building should be shifted enough several times a season to place the scratching shed over new soil, and the old soil spaded under, as the droppings cause the ground to become sour, which is detrimental to your flock. The board which is shown to screw on is for the purpose of separating the building readily and moving it in two sections.

The walls and roofs of this building may be put together with hooks and screw eyes, instead of being nailed together, but

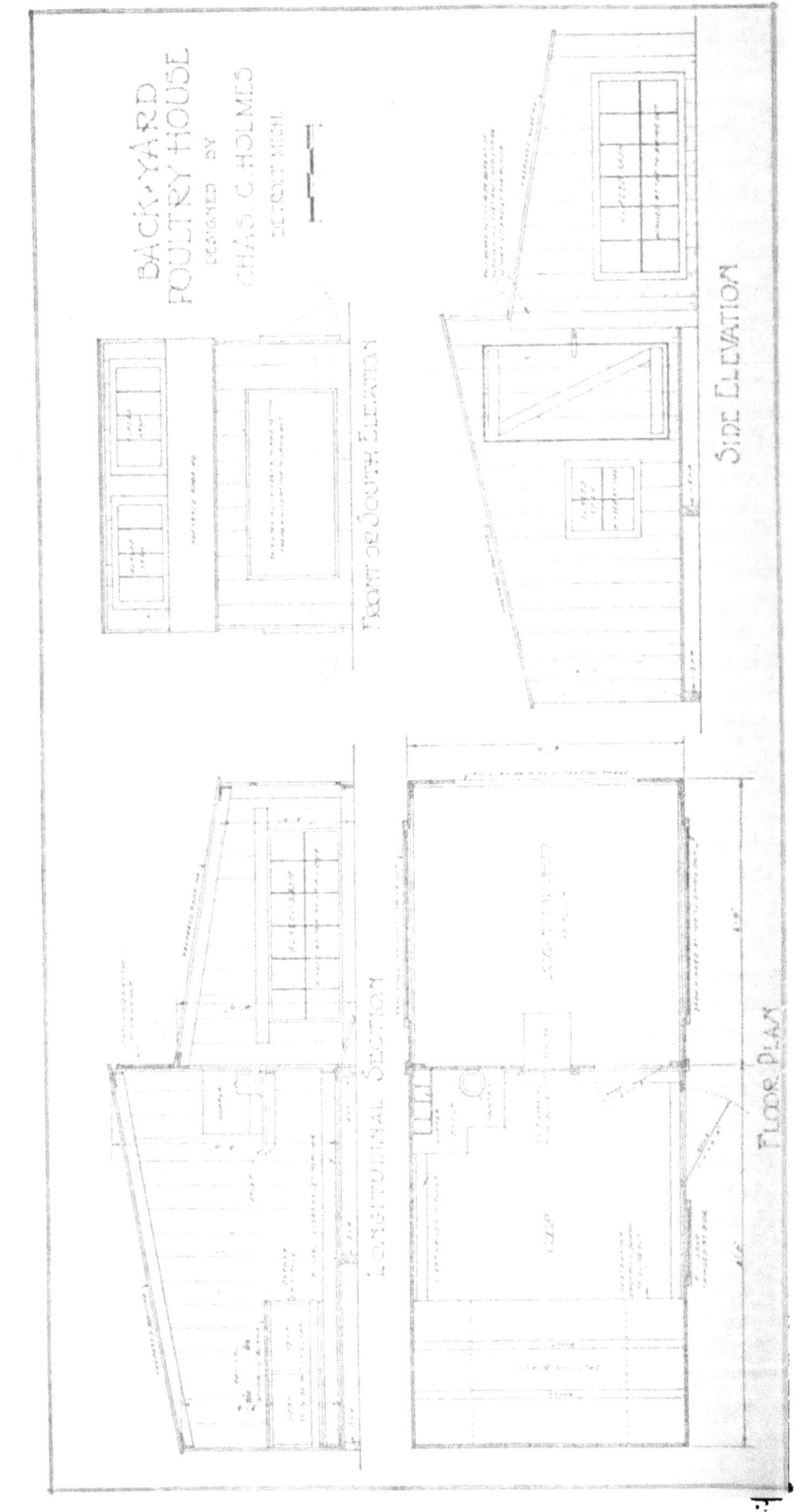

BACK-YARD
POULTRY HOUSE

DESIGNED BY
CHAS. C. HOLMES
DETROIT MICH.

FRONT OR SOUTH ELEVATION

SIDE ELEVATION

LONGITUDINAL SECTION

FLOOR PLAN

this is not necessary, however, unless you care to have it portable.

Don't overlook using a disinfecting white paint such as "Carbola" or white washing the entire interior of your building, as this is one of the most important things to be considered from a sanitary standpoint, as well as adding considerably to the light.

"A"-Shape Colony House.

The accompanying drawing illustrates a type of coop known as the "Colony House," but as this design is particularly adaptable to back yard poultry keeping, we will describe it briefly along this line for the benefit of those who are limited to the use of a city lot, where a larger building would be prohibitive. It will be noted that this building is shown to be constructed portable by the use of hinges or loose pinned butts and hooks. This construction is particularly good for those who wish to build one or more of these coops under shelter during the winter months, and place same at their selected location in the spring. The butts are to be screwed securely to cleats to hold the different sections tightly in place, and when ready to move or store away, the loose pins can be removed, leaving the butts in the proper location for erection. The entire coop is secured to the floor by the use of hooks and screw eyes, but should it be decided to locate the building permanently, the sections may be nailed together, which would, of course, eliminate the additional cost of hardware.

This coop being only eight feet square and supplied with plenty of glass to admit sunlight, it is especially adapted for limited space, where a scratching shed would cover too much ground. Altho matched flooring would make a tight and draft-proof building, it is a rather expensixe construction, so I would suggest a cheaper grade of lumber and cover the entire exterior of the coop with water-proof building paper.

It will be noticed that the dropping board does not extend the full width of the coop, allowing room to get at the back of the nests, but I believe I could improve on this by running the dropping board the full width of the coop and constructing nests to pull out on truck rollers or cleats. Another suggestion I would make, owing to the shallowness of this building, is this: Where the winters are severe I would provide a drop curtain in front of the roosts to eliminate as much as possible the freezing of the combs of the large-combed varieties.

Roosts are things that seem to be a matter of opinion among fanciers, but in my opinion it is natural for a chicken to stand

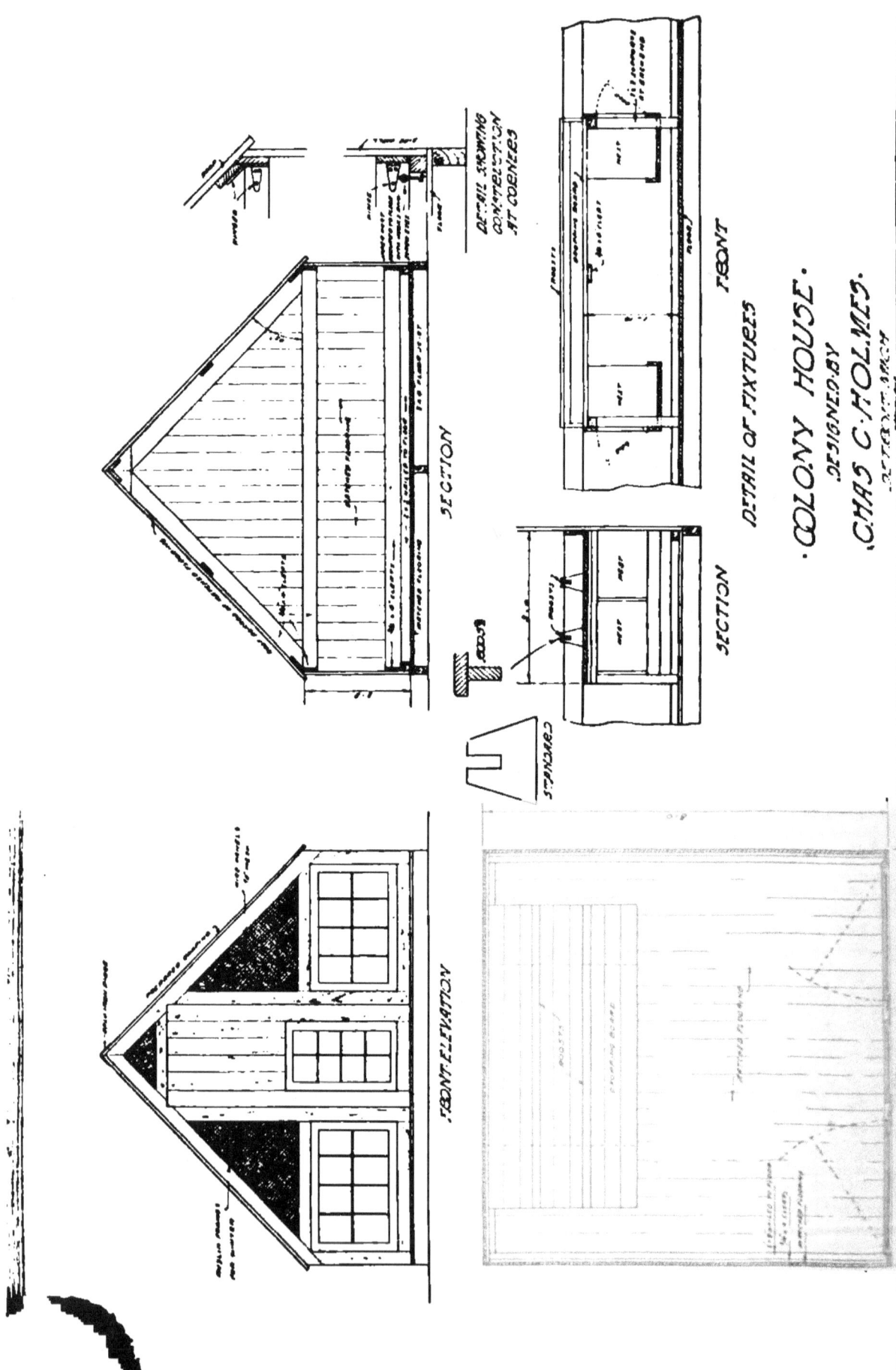

·COLONY HOUSE·
DESIGNED BY
·CHAS C·HOLMES·

flat-footed and not be obliged to cling to a round pole or narrow roost. I find the use of two strips about three inches wide, one being nailed edgewise to the other for stiffness forming a "T" shaped roost, to be very desirable and simple in construction.

Iowa Model of Half-Monitor Roof Type Poultry.

By H. A. BITTENBENDER, Professor in Poultry Husbandry, Iowa State College of Agriculture, Ames, Iowa.

The semi-monitor poultry house appears to be a good practical house for the general farm, because it contains those principles of construction which are essential for successful production. First of all it has the floor space arranged so that it will be most practical and beneficial for the poultry flock during the winter months. The principle of ventilation is maintained in the best possible manner. Sunlight can readily gain access in almost all parts of this house. Its cost, when compared with other types of houses is not much greater and for the few additional dollars that it may cost in construction it will pay good interest in the form of healthy poultry.

A few of the principles of poultry house construction which should be kept in mind are:

1. For 150 hens a house 22x24 is necessary.
2. The foundation of floor should consist of six to eight inches crushed stone or gravel, a layer of hollow tile and an inch of cement.
3. For every ten feet of floor space allow one foot of opening in front.
4. Face house toward south.
5. Windows in upper portion of house should be open four to six inches in winter and one to two feet in summer, hinged at bottom.

Poultry house construction is without doubt the most important factor in poultry management. Without a suitable poultry house it is impossible to obtain the most profit from the poultry flock. Disease and vermin are hard to control. The vitality is apt to be lowered and even with the most efficient ration good results cannot be hoped for. For these reasons we think that the first step after securing the right kind of stock is to provide suitable homes for the poultry flock.

The semi-monitor type of farm poultry house is not only economical in construction but its design fits in attractively with other farm buildings. These factors are not so essential to obtaining a high egg production, but when a house combines all of these essentials together with those for the development of the best health of the flock and a high and economical egg production, it is the best type of house to build.

The semi-monitor type of farm poultry house has been

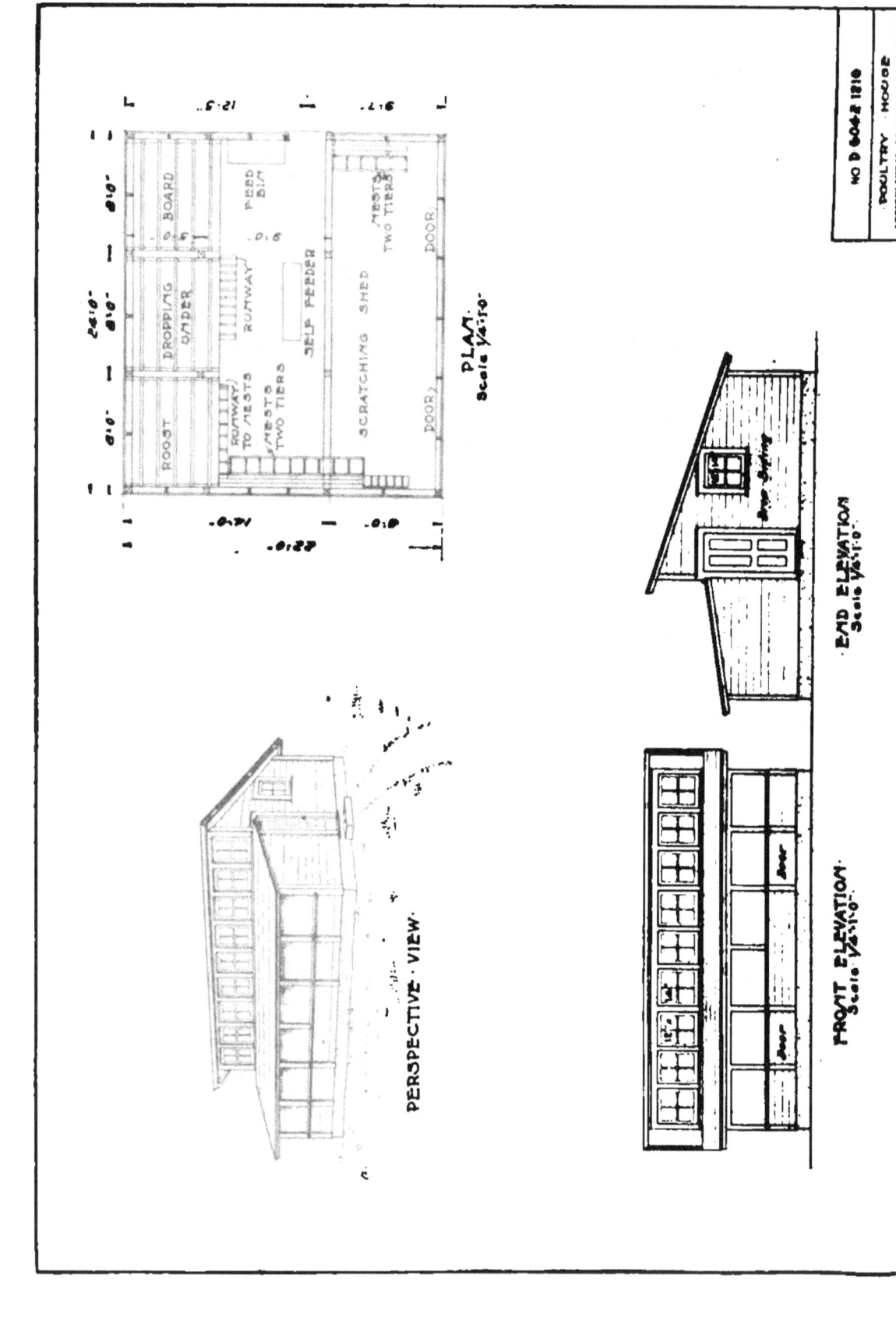

PLAN.
Scale ⅛ = 1'.0"

ROOST
DROPPING BOARD
RUNWAY TO NESTS
NESTS TWO TIERS
DOOR
FEED BIN
RUNWAY
SELF FEEDER
SCRATCHING SHED
NESTS TWO TIERS
DOOR

PERSPECTIVE · VIEW·

END ELEVATION
Scale ⅛ = 1'.0"

FRONT ELEVATION.
Scale ⅛ = 1'.0"

Door   Door

NO D 6042 1216
POULTRY HOUSE

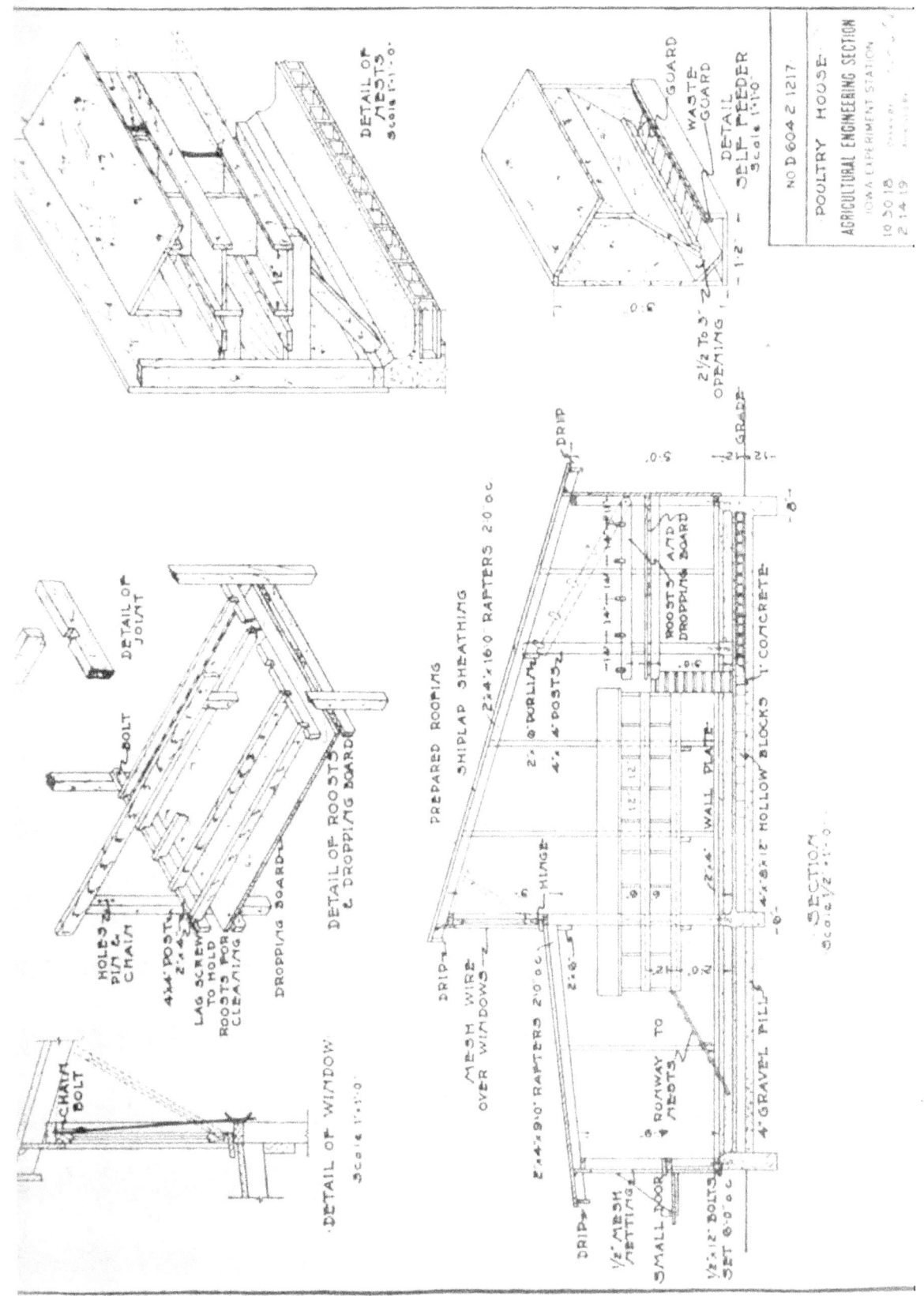

DETAIL OF NESTS
Scale 1"=1'-0"

DETAIL
SELF FEEDER
Scale 1"=1'-0"

GUARD
WASTE GUARD
2½" TO 3" OPENING
GRADE

NO D 604 Z 1217
POULTRY HOUSE
AGRICULTURAL ENGINEERING SECTION
IOWA EXPERIMENT STATION
10 50 18
2 14 19

DETAIL OF JOINT

BOLT

DETAIL OF ROOSTS
& DROPPING BOARD
Scale 1"=1'-0"

HOLES FOR PIN & CHAIN
4"4" POSTS 2"x4"
LAG SCREWS TO HOLD ROOSTS FOR CLEANING
DROPPING BOARD

DETAIL OF WINDOW
Scale 1"=1'-0"

CHAIN
BOLT

PREPARED ROOFING
SHIPLAP SHEATHING
2"x4"x16'0 RAFTERS 2'0 OC
2"x PURLIN
4"x4" POSTS

DRIP

ROOSTS AND DROPPING BOARD

MESH WIRE OVER WINDOWS
HINGE

2"x4"x9'0 RAFTERS 2'0 OC
2"x6"

DRIP
½" MESH NETTING
SMALL DOOR
½"x12" BOLTS SET 8'0 OC

RUNWAY TO NESTS

2"x4" WALL PLATE
4"x8"x12 HOLLOW BLOCKS CONCRETE

4" GRAVEL FILL

SECTION
Scale ½"=1'-0"

constructed in practically all parts of the country and it seems to work in equal success in the south as well as in the north. The depth of 22 feet with the arrangement of the windows and the open front, provides that almost the entire floor space of the house is reached by sunlight at some time during the day. Especially during the winter months when the days are short is the sunlight at its best from the standpoint of this house.

For extreme northern conditions, if the open front covered with muslin frames proves too severe, part of the front can be equipped with windows but only in a few instances has this been found necessary.

The house is complete in practically every detail. The roosts are hinged at the back and can be raised for cleaning, the dropping board slides in and is easily removed for thoro disinfection. With all of these conveniences it takes but little time to care for a flock of 150 chickens. This unit of construction should be kept in mind and if the flock desired is more than 150, add to the length of the house but do not change the depth or height of the house, as it has been found that these dimensions produce the desired results.

Agricultural Extension Poster No. 18, issued by the Iowa State College of Agriculture gives detailed plans of the Iowa Model House.

A Cheap Scratching Shed.

In spite of all the precaution not to have too many fowls in a house a great many poultrymen find that their houses are too small to comfortably accommodate the flock which they would like to keep over. On account of being over crowded quite a number of poultrymen have found that their hens do not lay in November as they should when the price of eggs goes soaring. Hens can't possibly do well if they are crowded or are not fed right. The feed is a great factor in getting eggs but no matter how perfect the feed or well balanced the ration the hens will not lay unless they have comfortable quarters, cozy roosts, fresh air and plenty of litter to exercise in.

Even if it is December and winter, if your hens are not laying as they should and are overcrowded it is not too late to build a shed like the sketch, on the side of the poultry house or barn. Have the lumber and roofing material all ready and the first nice day two men can put up a shed like this in a very short time. If the ground is frozen so that you cannot put a lot of gravel in it, fill it with cinders so the shed will not be damp on the floor. I would not advise putting in a wooden floor unless you have a lot of cheap waste lumber, but then if you do this you will have to take care to build it high enough so that it will not be a harbor for rats and if it is built up off the ground the wind sweeping under it is liable to make it cold.

Don't make the mistake of making this shed too high. The lower it is the more comfortable. With a suitable roofing material the slant of the roof need not be very great.

Leave the whole south side of this shed open. It may be covered with wire netting as it a good idea to keep the hens

A cheap scratching shed.

confined in the house, where a shed for scratching is provided, the greater part of the cold winter months. Some of the weaker fowls cannot then be driven out in the cold wind and take cold or roup as is so often the case.

The secret of making the hens happy, like a boy, is to give them something to do and the only way to keep the hens busy in cold winter months when everything is frozen up, is to provide plenty of litter. You can hardly provide too much nice clean straw for a hen to scratch in. Many farmers wonder why their hens do not lay during the winter and yet they have plenty of the wherewith with which to make the hen happy and keep her busy.

Into the litter of straw some six or eight inches deep feed all the whole grains and make the hens work for as much of their feed as possible.

A California Poultry House.

Chickens thrive most and do best where they can roam about over green fields and under the orchard and woodland shade at will, searching for the morsel that strikes their particular fancy. To keep the fowls close to nature is the secret of success of many of our most famous fanciers and exhibitors. Even when it comes to conditioning for show purposes the secret of success of many a string of blue ribbon winners has been that they were left to roam here and there, but with careful attention and extra morsels of food placed in inviting places each day, and the fowls thus left round out their bodies and fill out their plumage until almost the last day before the show.

The California poultry house.

This brings a fowl in in what is termed "the pink of condition," which cannot be beaten by any amount of unnatural conditioning. When they are housed unnaturally and pampered they soon show a lack of vitality.

The canvas front and open air types of houses have solved the problem for the poulterers in the northern states, but it was left for the California poulterers to adapt a different style of architecture entirely in poultry house construction, and the type of house shown in the illustration is the product of California same as the bungalow.

This house is used quite extensively upon some of the large Leghorn egg-laying farms. These houses are distributed out over the orchard or almond grove, and units of thirty or forty hens roost in a house. The fowls kept in this fashion are as near to nature as it is possible to keep them. They do much better when kept in small flocks as it seems to be nature's plan to have small flocks and abhore great masses. The houses are far enough apart that it is not necessary to place wire netting between them. The fowls, of course, run together somewhat during the day, but large numbers of them are never found congregated together in one place.

It will be noticed that their roosts are rather high and on a level. The higher the roost for the Leghorn, the better as it seems to give them an air of security and contentment. The highest roost, you have always noticed with fowls, is always the choicest place according to chicken idea, and so they are all placed on a level, eliminating crowding in one part of the house.

Making the Poultry House Burglar Proof.

It is a safe maximum to say: "That the higher class the home and its out buildings and the better the stock and possessions the more liable they are to be tampered with and invaded by thieves." No matter where you are situated, you are running a risk of having the horse stolen, the barn burned, or the hen roost lifted, however remote the risk might seem to you. And by the way, had you ever noticed that the person who rests so secure persuaded to believe he is by his own reasoning, is the one first touched by thieves. Like the farmer of old, they are the ones who lock the barn after the horse is gone.

For the want of reliable information on the subject and because the average electrician does not make a business of putting in burglar alarms and therefore does not keep posted on the latest methods of putting them in the average property owner has been led to think the cost of installing one is rather heavy and the systems too complicated to work well and be absolutely reliable under all circumstances in untrained hands.

There are two systems of wiring—the open and the closed. The open circuit system is used much more than the closed altho the closed is the more reliable in some respects. In the open circuit system all that is required is two dry cell batteries, a bell and the insulated wire is arranged in the building so that if a window or door is opened it will cause the wire running from the batteries to be connected and thus ring the bell. Most anyone with any knowledge of electrical appliances at all can install the open circuit system for the doors and windows of the home. The weak point about the open circuit is that it is easy to put out of commission by the ordinary thief if it is installed in the barn or poultry house with the wires running to the house. The thief will be almost sure to see these wires and with an ordinary pen knife cut one or both and thus opening the open circuit all the wider and cutting off all chance of the two ends of the wire meeting and completing the circuit and ringing the bell in the house. But if the wires can be put in an underground conduit or concealed so they cannot possibly be discovered the open circuit is just as reliable in any of the outbuildings as in the home. With the closed circuit, which will be described later, the thief gets himself into trouble all the sooner by cutting the wires and it is advisable with this system to put them in plain view for just the moment the circuit is broken by the wire being cut the bell immediately rings in the house. And no matter how expert the thief he cannot experiment with the wires on the outside of a building to find whether they connect an open or closed system without setting the bell to ringing if the closed system is used. The closed system is so seldom used that he will most likely sever the wire. I say this is the most likely thing he will do. Nine chances to one it is an open system and then nine chances to one he has put the electric alarm system out of commission in short order but if yours is the tenth chance and the closed circuit trouble is on hand at once.

The Open Circuit.

The open circuit needs an electric bell with a 2½ inch gong and enough annunciator, or bell wire, to make a metallic circuit to your residence. Rubber covered heavier wire is preferable for outside wiring. Two cells of dry battery should operate a distance of two hundred feet and an additional cell for each hundred feet. To wire a poultry house or barn, on the sill of

Showing plate under door for open system. When a person steps on the board the contact is made on the copper plates between the board and sill.

each opening tack a piece of copper tin 2x4 inches, every two feet. Under this tin plate, coil a piece of wire, free from insulation for two or more inches so that the tin will press firmly against the bare bright wire. Then saw a board the width of your sill and about one inch shorter at each end than the opening to fit over the sill. Mark on the board where the tin plate will strike this board, if placed in its proper place and place tin or copper with two feet of wire attached, on the board the same as on the sill. Now get some No. 1 brass spring wire and make three or four springs about one inch high when opened enough to spring good. Bore holes in the sill and the board to match about one-quarter inch in depth and fit the springs in them. Placed thus, they should keep the square pieces of contact plates about one-quarter inches apart. Bore four holes thru the top board a little larger than a good sized wire spike. Then set the board in its proper position with springs under and drive spikes in the holes down until the heads leave about one-quarter in play at the top above the board. This allows the board to work up and down if pressure is made on the board at any point and yet the board is firmly attached to the sill so that it cannot be detached easily.

The two wires brought from the residence attached to the fence posts and the outbuildings and carried along under the brought inside the wired building and carried along under the windows and past the doors. Each wire of the upper contact boards is connected with one of the wires from the residence from the sill are connected with the other wire from the residence. Care must be taken to remove the insulation from the wire wherever a connection is made.

Plates or boards as described above should be placed under or on the sills of all the windows and doors but as an extra precaution for the doors where the thief is liable to be careful not to step on the sill, tack a piece of tin or copper two inches square on the back edge with the bare end of the wire under it the same as under the sills. On the weather-boarding place a piece of the spring wire about two inches long with an eye at one end for a heavy screw. Then fasten a short insulated wire, ends scraped off, to the screw, running it (the wire) thru the board and into the building. The wires attached to the tin on the door and the screw on the spring should be attached to the wires leading to the residence, the same as the sill connections. If the door opens inwardly it is much better as the connection is on the inside where it cannot be tampered with. Now when you lock your house at night turn the spring on door over the tin plate just so it will not touch unless door is opened. The connections on the sills are always set so that the door is all that need be bothered with each night. Now fasten your bell where wanted in the house, attaching one wire from the wired building to one binding post on the bell, and the other wire from the building to the zinc post of nut attachment on the outer edge of one battery. With a small piece of wire attach the center post of this same battery to the zinc of the second battery and the carbon center post of this battery to the other binding post on the bell. The system is complete and the moment pressure is applied on the sill in the poultry house or barn bell gives the warning.

The Closed System.

The closed system is much more complicated and therefore costs more to install but when once installed it will last for years and will operate clear across a town, if wired properly, and is absolutely dependable. The batteries are strong enough with this system that the house and all the outbuildings can be wired and attached to the same circuit. The closed circuit is really two circuits. The electricity is continually flowing thru one thus causing an iron bar (in the telegraph relay) to be magnetized continually so that it holds another iron bar firmly

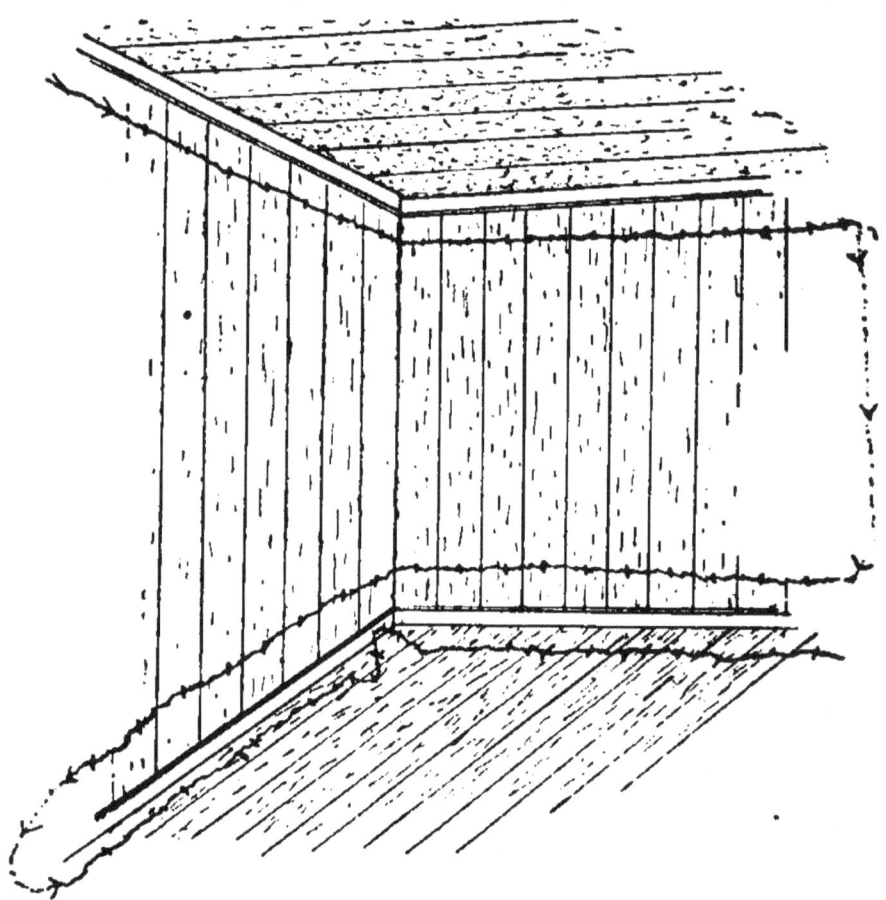

Showing method of tacking wire on each board in roof and side to prevent thieves removing boards. For closed circuit and wet batteries only.

to it, immediately when the wire is cut or the circuit broken the iron bar loses its magnetism and drops the other iron bar and this bar in dropping completes the circuit on another system and it rings the bell just as in the open circuit.

It takes the following material to make the closed circuit system:

1 telegraph relay, either Pony or main line.
I two point switch.
6 jars crow foot batteries.

Main line covered telephone wire for all outside wiring.

Annunciator wire for inside work.

Porcelain knobs if you run wire outside on posts, otherwise staple it but do not break the insulation.

Blue vitrol.

1 small door bell, electric same as open circuit.

1 two-point switch.

2 dry batteries. (The last three items are required for the bell circuit inside the house.)

With the closed circuit it requires six wet batteries beside the two dry ones. Each work independently of each other, or rather their circuits do not connect. Set up the six wet batteries a couple of days before using as follows: Take the copper plates furnished with the wet batteries, open them out and bend ends over a trifle and place one in the bottom of each jar. Hang the zinc crow foot on the edge of each jar and then carefully fill the jar with water until the water covers the prongs

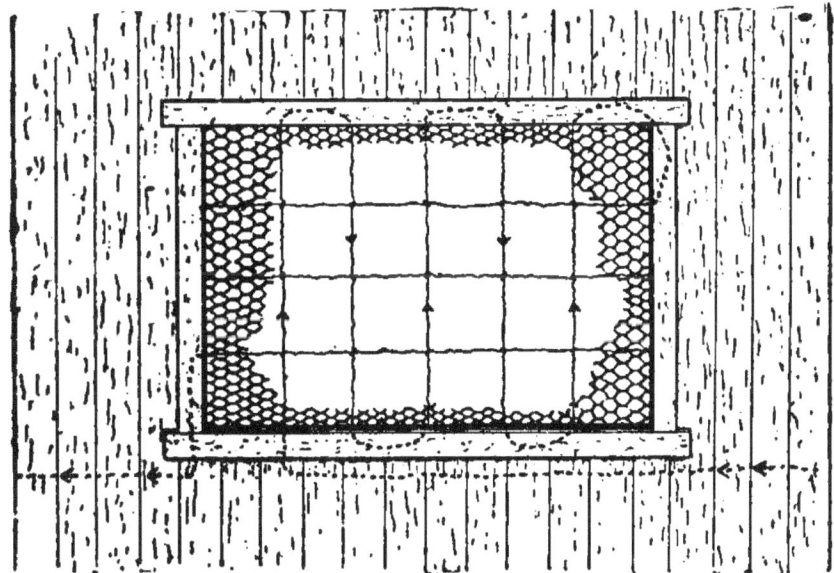

Method of weaving insulated wire in wire netting or back of canvas in the fresh air style of poultry house so widely used at the present time. The moment a thief cuts the wire the bell rings.

of the crow foot. Connect up the batteries with short pieces of copper wire by attaching the copper of one jar to the zinc of the other and so on thru the six jars and finally connect the copper with the sixth one to the zinc of the first one and let them work 48 hours.

Put the wet batteries in the cellar or some out of the way place where they will not freeze. Place the relay up on a shelf where it will not be disturbed. Run a wire from one of the binding posts on the relay to the copper plate of the first bat-

tery. Run a wire from the other binding post of the relay to
the poultry house, placing a two-point switch in it at some convenient point about the house so it can be opened and closed at
will. From the crow foot on the last wet battery run a second
wire to the poultry house. Two wires are attached to the other
two binding posts of the relay and one is attached to the center
post of one of the dry batteries. The zinc of the first dry battery is attached to the center post of the second dry battery by

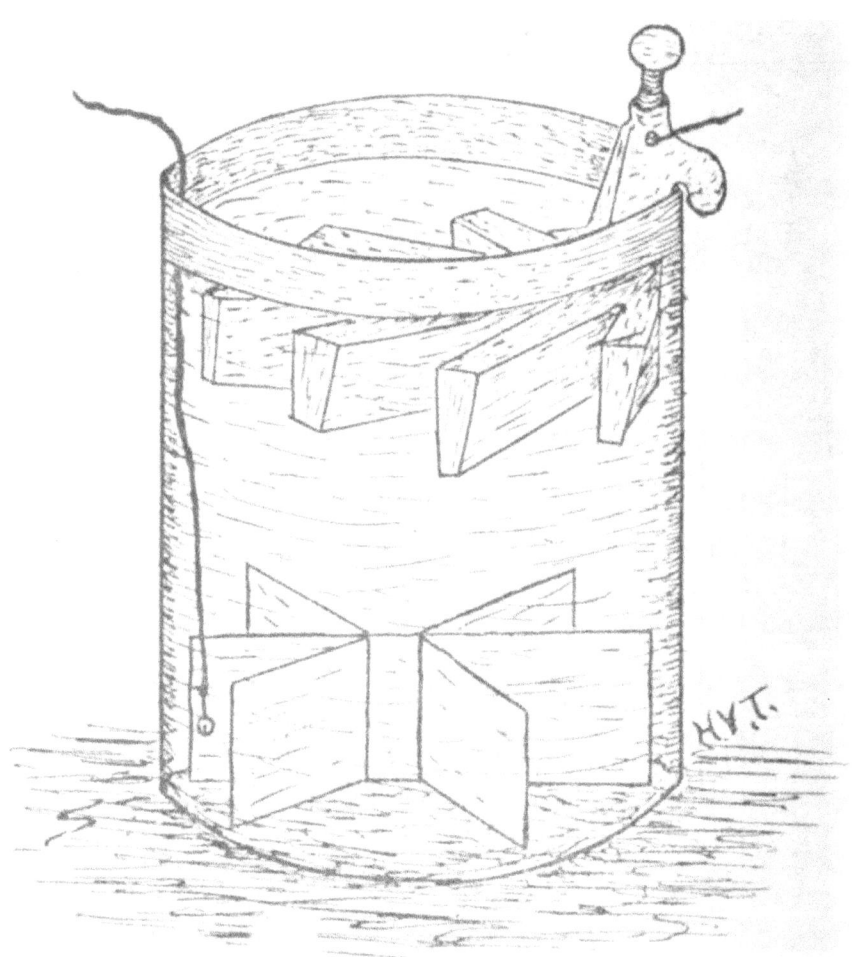

A wet battery crow-foot kind. Six of these are required for the close
circuit alarm.

a small wire and a wire from the zinc of the second batter
run to the small bell in the bedroom and attached to one of
binding posts. Run the second wire from the binding post 1
thru a two-point switch to the relay. Then as stated ab
when the current is running thru the wet battery sysem it k
the dry battery system open but the moment the wet battery

cuit is cut or opened it releases the open battery circuit, closing it and ringing the bell. As might be expected, then, with the wet battery or closed system, the houses have to be wired exactly opposite so that the circuit is complete all the time. Instead of springs to keep the points of contact apart, as in the open circuit, springs should be used to keep the contact plates together all the time so that the moment they are tampered with, the window opened or door opened, they fly apart.

The advantage with the closed circuit is that the wire can be tacked to each board on the back, sides and roof of a poultry house, if there is any danger of thieves removing the boards to get in, as they quite often do, and then when a board is pried off the thief breaks or cuts the wire causing his undoing. If the small insulated wire is securely stapled to each board in the back and sides of the barn or poultry house the prying off of the first board will easily break the wire and the thief will probably not know anything about it, and you can dress at liesure and then yet get to the building before he has pried off enough boards to get in.

Another decided advantage of the closed system is that the house to be wired for thieves need not be closed tight. In the case of a poultry house it may be an open front with only wire netting covering the opening or it may be that the openings are covered with canvas or muslin in which case they can be wired just as easily as the closed building. If a barn is wired and several windows are to to be left open during the summer a covering of wire netting is all that is necessary. Use the small insulated bell wire in this case and across any opening weave it in and out in the wire netting across the opening at intervals of eight inches or a foot. Then connecting with the same wire weave it, likewise, up and down across the opening, thus making squares eight inches or one foot in diameter. With a canvas front poultry house the wires should be tacked across in the same manner just back of the canvas. In either case be sure the wire is securely fastened on the sills each time so it will require cutting to get it loose. The thief will hardly notice the wire if woven in with the wire netting and he will not lose much time in cutting it after cutting the canvas front or wire netting.

Even with closed windows this same method of running the wire back and forth across the opening just back of the window and fastening it to the sill each time, may be employed. The window may be opened or closed at will and yet the system is always ready. Where a window is always closed at night or opened a certain distance (being sure the distance is not enough to admit a man's body without raising it higher) two points of contact may be made by imbedding a copper plate in the window frame and one in the window just opposite so that they press firmly against each other. When the window is raised these points of contact are pulled apart, thus breaking the current and ringing the bell. A copper plate may be imbedded in the door and door frame in the same manner so that they press firmly against each other when the door is closed. When the door is opened, then, the current is broken. So easy is it to set up a closed circuit system and have it work that a wood pile might be wired in a few minutes time. Two sticks of wood, which would most likely be picked up should have the ends of the insulated wire fastened to them. The insulation is cut off in a convenient place on each stick and then the sticks placed on the pile of wood so the bare wires of each stick press against each other and form a firm contact. When the current is turned on it flows through this break uninterrupted. But when one of the sticks is picked up or moved the current is broken and the bell rings.

During the day when the system is not in use the switches

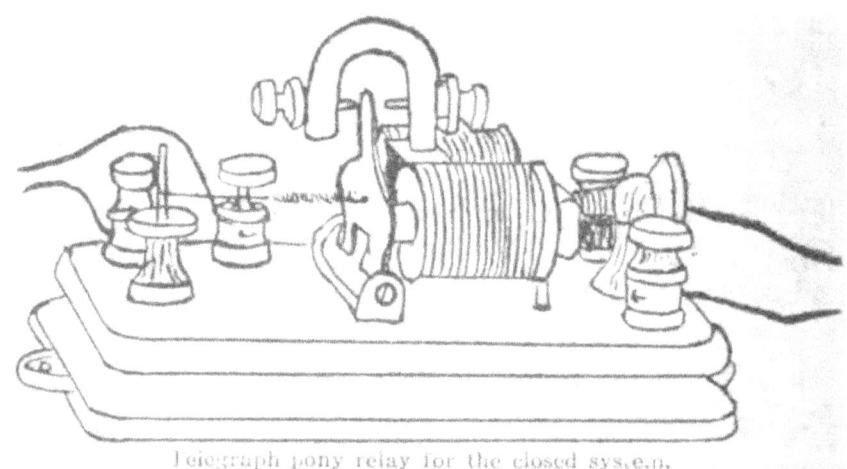

Telegraph pony relay for the closed system.

leading each way from the relay and controlling the dry and wet battery circuits should be opened so the wet batteries wil' not be working and wasting continually.

The wet batteries are cheaper to keep up after once installe¢ than the dry ones. They should be cleaned about every tw months and half of the old solution used again. The crow-foo should always be covered with water to insure it working prop erly.

Follow the following instructions in adjusting the relaj which can be purchased of any electrical store:

Reverse the back contact screw so that the platinum poir will be in front of the armature and the rubber point scre' over the magnets. The relay must be adjusted close up to th armature. These terms will be easy to understand if the rela is in hand. The electrician, though, in a moment's time, ca explain the working of it. The relay is similar to the ticker ¢

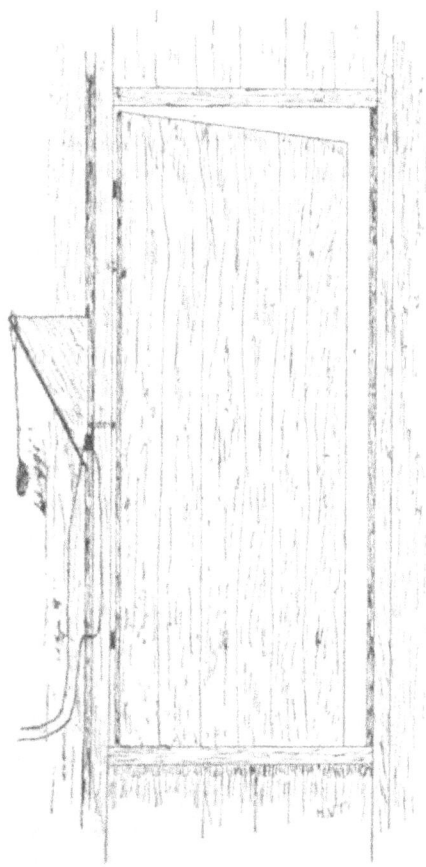

With the triangular piece of board hinged at the top as shown and a spike nail or iron bolt fitting in a hole in the door jam on the hinged side, a contact is made by opening the door. When the door is closed the contact is broken. Can be made in ten minutes for the open or dry battery circuit.

a telegraph instrument but it does not have the telegraph key attached. They can be purchased for various sums, but the cheapest will answer the purpose well.

The closed circuit system is generally used in wiring jewelers show cases and windows and doors and homes with private collections or rare and costly collections of gems or books or what not. But because the information is not given out how to install it by electricians, generally, it is not as extensively used as is the open circuit which can be installed by most anyone today. They are so simple that the average school boy can set them up and the knowledge of how to operate them is not and cannot be kept in the hands of the expert electricians.

All owners of valuable stock, poultry or outbuildings should install the closed circuit and have all fear of thieves allayed. For the home, only, the open circuit described first is the better and cheaper.

Automatic Release Door.

Poultry breeders who are believers in the old adage: "The early bird gets the worm," will undoubtedly be interested in the accompanying illustration of an automatic release door to be used on poultry houses where it is desired that the poultry shall be securely locked during the night and yet have the advantage of the first rays of the morning sun out on the range. The flock out on the range with the first rays of daylight has the advantage of two or three of the best hours of the day to grow and to find the early bugs and worms which they would not otherwise have, should they have to sit and fret waiting for their keeper to release the trap door to let them out to freedom and the fresh morning air.

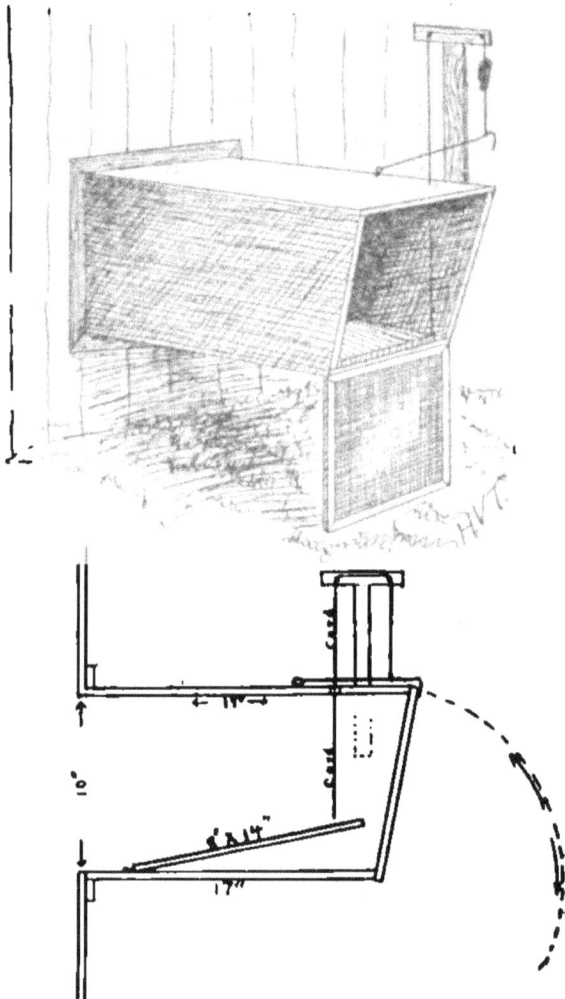

Those who have had the sad experience of the nightly raids upon their hen roosts, by weasels, foxes or other night prowlers, when the house was left open for the fowls to get out bright and early will especially welcome these plans.

Automatic release door.

An explanation of the plans is hardly necessary as the sketch well gives the details of construction. The movement of the trap is very simple and easy and is released by the first bird which walks onto the slightly raised false floor. A string is fastened to this floor passing up over the projecting T-shape attachment and down to the wire hook. To this cord is attached a weight, heavy enough to balance the false floor when raised and set for action as shown in the lower plan. The trap is attached to the outside of the building and can be of any size desired according to the breed. The dimensions given are suitable for any of the medium sized fowls, but for any of the large ones, such as Brahmas, Cochins, or Langshans, the opening into the house will have to be enlarged accordingly.

The front trap door is covered with inch mesh wire netting or the finer one-half inch if it is desired to be sure of the weasels. This door must be covered with wire that the fowls may be attracted by the light and thus be induced to come out upon the false floor and release themselves. When the wire door is up the hook is pulled down over the edge and should be tight enough to hold on by its own weight, as all resistence is relieved by the counter weight which is fastened just above the hook. The weight, of course, should be just heavy enough to balance the false floor, so that it will stand in any position to which it may be raised.

About four inches is sufficient incline to set the false floor. The end of the false floor toward the building should be fastened to the floor with a hinge. The weight of the first hen will release the trap door the instant she walks out upon the inclined board permitting all the flock to pass out.

A Good Home Made Trapnest.

The illustration shown gives a fair idea of a trap nest that anybody can make in a little while with only a hammer and a saw for tools. Of course, if you have many hens you will have to make several nests to accommodate all, and then all the other nests must be closed or torn up.

The trap nest has been quite an important factor in building up strains of heavy layers among most of the popular breeds today. The down-to-date American has insisted upon knowing just how many eggs a hen could lay in a year when the statement was made that she was a good layer. Then with definite figures and a standard to go by, made by the best layers in a large flock, he has insisted that it was possible to have a whole flock of layers as capable of turning out a great number of eggs as the few heavy layers that he started with. What the Babcock test has done for the dairyman in eliminating the non-cream producing cows from his herd, the trap nest has done for poultrydom in eliminating the non-layers from the flock of hens. Using the trap nest. the breeder, by a process of elimination and culling each year, breeds from only the best layers in his flock and has slowly increased the average egg yield per hen until it is a third more than twenty-five years ago. The small fancier and back-yard poultry raiser has taken more interest and has been more successful along this line, as he has had only a few hens and a limited space. He knew just how many hens he had and how many his neighbor had and the neighborly pride in getting more eggs per hen from his flock excited more care and interest.

The trap nest is made in two compartments. The box proper is fifteen inches square by thirty-two to thirty-six inches long. The hole or opening between the compartments need not be round as pictured unless you care to make it so, but it should be just large enough for a hen from your flock to pass through easily. The larger breeds require a larger opening, of course.

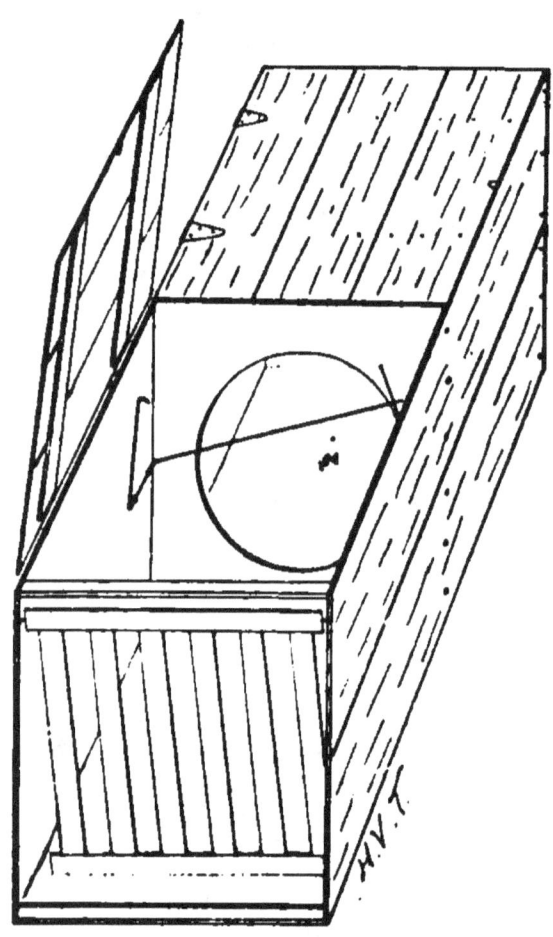

Home made Trap Nest, described by H. V. Tormohlen in accompanying article.

A large stiff wire is bent in the shape indicated, and the part passing over the opening is made to work freely up and down under the wire guards held by small staples, the whole wire assuming a lever action.

With the trap door caught up on other arm of the lever, the hen passes under it and as she starts to pass under the wire lever into the second compartment and into the nest proper, her back gently presses against the wire raising it and at the same instant sliding the other end of the lever out from under the trap door. The first compartment should be made a little longer than the trap door is high enough to prevent the door dropping on the hen's back before she gets quite into the nest proper. The wire arm over the opening should be placed high enough so that the hen will naturally try to pass under it instead of over it. Each hen should have an aluminum or copper leg band, with a number on it, on one of her legs. Then as you release the hen you can put the egg down on your memorandum to her credit. Sometimes the hens will enter the nest for curiosity, and especially is this true when the system is first installed, but after they become used to it, they will seldom ever enter except to lay. To get the hens acquainted with the nests the doors may be propped up for several days.

The trap is also excellent for sitting hens—you can release the hen to get her feed and trap the door, and then after she goes back on her nest she shuts the door after her and other hens cannot enter to bother her or break the eggs. You can also easily catch the hen that is an egg eater with the trap nest, as some of the broken egg shells will tell the tale.

A Simple Home Made Trapnest.

This illustration shows a simple trapnest that can easily be made by anyone handy with tools. It can be made out of any ordinary box with the proper dimensions. The complete nest should be about eighteen inches long and the front about one foot square. A strip about two inches wide should be fastened on the floor of the nest about twelve inches from the back, mak-

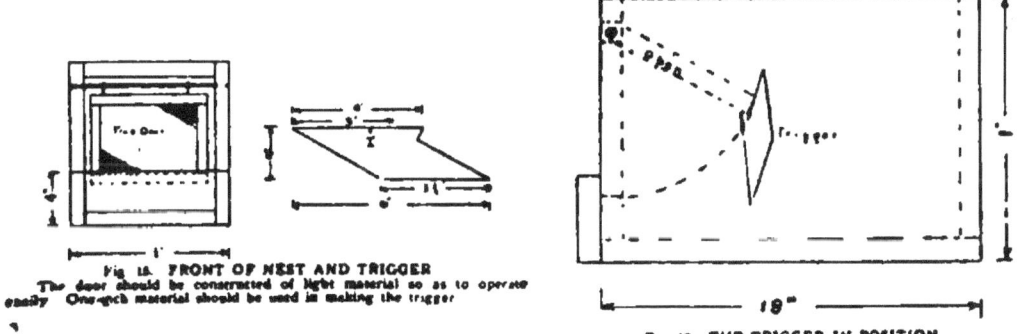

Fig. 18 FRONT OF NEST AND TRIGGER
The door should be constructed of light material so as to operate easily. One-inch material should be used in making the trigger

Fig. 19 THE TRIGGER IN POSITION
The dotted lines show the open door. When raised by the hen entering the trigger is released allowing door to fall shut

ing a nest in the back of the box about twelve inches square. The trigger, which is made out of one-inch material, is fastened to the side of the nest box. When the trap is set the door rests on this trigger. As the hen enters, she raises the door slightly with her back, thus releasing the trigger, which drops down, permitting the door to close as the hen continues to enter the nest. This nest is one of the simplest and most satisfactory trapnests that can be made at home.

The False Floor Trapnest.

False floor trap nest.

There are many ways of making trapnests, some of them more or less complicated and depending upon the various triggers, springs, trips, etc., but the one shown in the illustration is about as simple as any made. The disadvantage this nest has is that the nest material is liable to interfere with the working of the false floor upon which it rests and also is liable to get under the false floor and keep it from dropping down under the weight of hen as it should. For this reason it would not be pronounced the best trapnest devised but it may be classed as one of the simplest and easiest made.

All that is necessary to make this nest is an oblong box into which a light board the size of the floor is fitted. Onto this board is tacked a light inch strip underneath so the board will balance on it. Then a lever or upright bracket is nailed on so that it will barely hold the door up as shown in the cut. When the hen walks into the nest and passes back past the balance plate her weight pulls the lever back out from under the door and thus it falls into place and holds the hen until she has laid the coveted egg and been credited with same by the keeper.

Nesting Boxes.

As many nests as desired may be constructed in one section. The illustration herewith shows four. For Leghorns, place the partitions twelve inches apart and for the larger breeds fourteen inches. Nail the partitions only to the roof or top and to the three-inch strip in front, leaving the bottom loose. The wall of the house forms the back of the nests. They should be set against it and not fastened, thus making them easily removable for cleaning Braces for holding the nests should be fastened against the

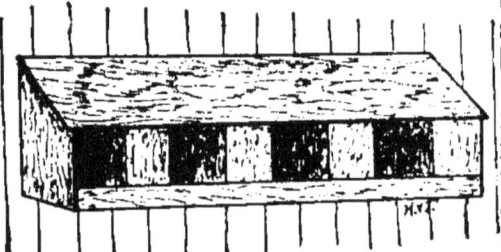

wall as shown. If nests are much above the floor of the house the bottom board should be six inches beyond them in front to form a platform upon which the fowls can fly when getting into the nests.

Troughs for Fowls.

During the rainy days of spring or even while it is yet too cold to do much work outside the thoughtful poultryman will

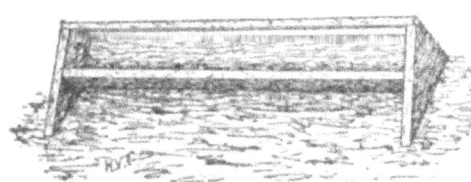

anticipate his needs in troughs and fountains for his breeding pens and for the many chicks he is going to hatch. During these days while in doors many conveniences like the one illustrated may be made. Have

Home made feeding trough.

them on hand when the rush is on and when you will have time only to steal out a pie pan from the kitchen to feed the new chicks on if you haven't made enough troughs and feeders.

Cement Nests for Hens.

The steady rise in the price of lumber and the ever-increasing scarcity of good lumber has made the impetus of the cement age all the more pronounced. The encouraging feature about the gloomy lumber situation has been, though. that cement, as a general thing, has been found superior, in nearly every respect to lumber. Nearly everything about the farm which was formerly built out of lumber is or can now be constructed from cement. Barns, troughs, tanks, mangers, floors and bins and what not built of cement are much more satisfactory than frame. The up-to-date poultry raiser has not been far behind in acknowledging the superiority of cement for poultry house construction. With cement floors they are much warmer in winter and cooler in summer. They are much more sanitary and easier to clean and they are rat and vermin proof. The time is not far distant when we will possibly have cement dropping boards and nests built with the cement walls of our hen houses, but thus far this has not been found practical on account of the bulkiness of the cement and the vast amount of tedious work and small moulds it would take for a house of any considerable dimensions.

The hens should be discouraged in laying in the hen house during the hot summer months, anyway, providing plenty of cool nests are provided out about the premises. The laying and setting hens will find more comfort in these nests and the lice and mites are much easier to combat.

The advantage of the cement nests for outdoor use is that they are practically indestructible, they are cool, they do not harbor rats, and they do not easily become infested with lice—they can be burnt out in a few moment's time and you are sure every nit and louse has been destroyed.

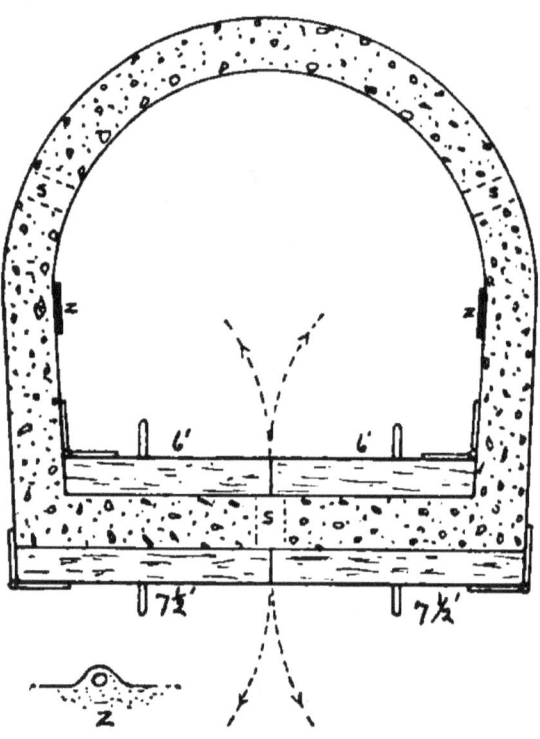

The accompanying sketch and drawings show a method for making a cement hen's nest. The inner and outer forms consist of galvanized sheet iron (No. 15 B. & S. gauge). hinged to 1 inch boards for the bottom, which are hooked together as shown when the mould is closed ready to be filled.

For the outer form a piece of sheet iron 41 inches long and 15½ in. wide is required, and for the inner form a piece 29 inches long and 14 inches wide. Two loops are cut in the galvanized iron or riveted on to one end of the mould and marked x in the drawing. These are placed directly opposite each other as shown, so that a stick or rod can be passed through them. When in position this stick rests upon the outer form and holds the inner form up 1½ inches from the back as the nest forms are placed on end while be-

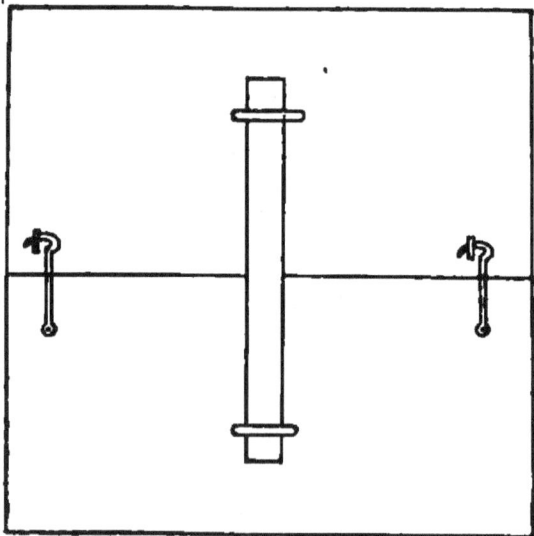

Plans of the wooden base and the shell necessary in making cement nests as described.

ing filled with cement. The wooden base for the inner form consists of two 1 inch boards 6 inches long, and for the outer forms of two 1 inch boards 7½ inches long and 15½ inches long. These wooden bases are prevented from bending at the joint by placing a small strip or rod in under the brackets.

The concrete should be composed of 1 part cement to not more than 4 parts sand or bank run gravel with no particles coarser than ½-inch. The mixture should be of such consistency as will require a slight amount of tamping to force it to all parts of the mould.

The outer form is first placed in position (on end) on a wooden pallet or floor and 1½ inches of concrete then deposited. The inner form, with sticks thru parts z, is then set in position and three pieces of wood 1½ inches wide (s in diagram) and 14 inches long are placed between the inner and outer forms to act as spacers.

The concrete is then deposited, and when the mould is half full the spacers are removed. The mould is then filled and removed to a cool, moist place to cure for seven days. At the end of twenty-four hours the moulds can be removed, care being taken not to knock off any corners. With a few moment's spare time each day with one mould enough nests can be made to have enough nests out doors to accommodate all the hens during the warm months. The nest can be placed under bushes and in out of the way places and the hens will enjoy them much more than being crowded in the hen house. The hens will not be so apt to hide their nests, either, when the nests are put in secluded and shady places.

Cement nest as it appears when ready for use.

A Common Sense Window for Fresh Air Poultry Houses.

A few years ago it was quite general among our farmers and poultry raisers to plaster the walls of their coops and furnish artificial heat to induce their chickens to produce more in the winter months, but in recent years we have learned through experience that plenty of fresh air at all times is one of the most essential factors in successful poultry raising.

Our agricultural colleges are teaching the raising of poultry successfully with the use of fresh air poultry houses, the government is advocating the use of fresh air poultry houses in their bulletins, and uses them extensively at their experimental stations, and the most successful poultry raisers in the country are using the fresh air type of houses.

Vigor and hardiness combined with proper feeding are what have brought the productiveness of our fowl to the maximum today, and without plenty of dry, fresh air we have neither

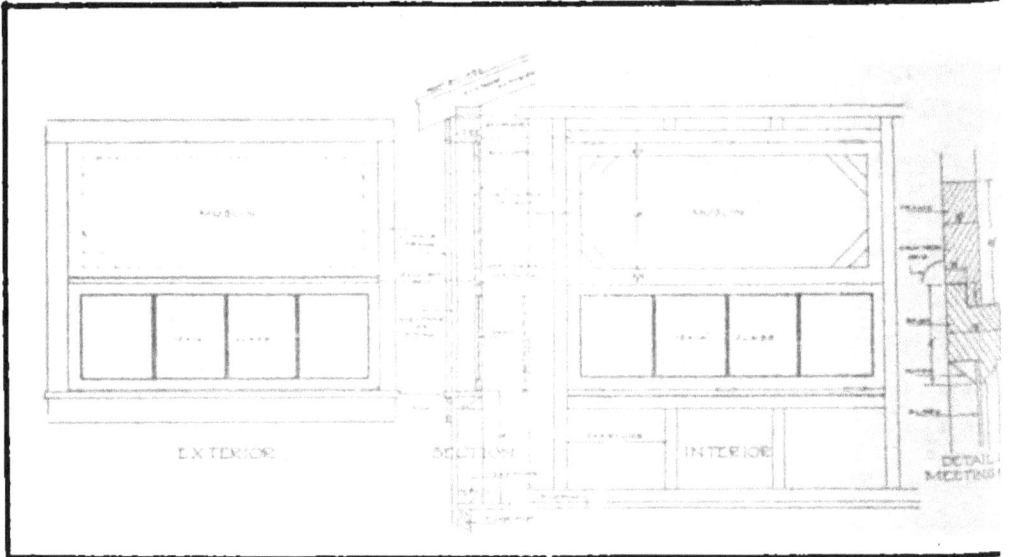

the vigor nor the hardiness, and wonder why our flock is not as productive as the flock kept under modern methods or favorable conditions.

We will not go into detail on feeding in this article, but will adhere to the necessity of fresh air, and show our friend what we mean by fresh air construction with these drawings which I have prepared as simply as possible so the man with the least mechanical ingenuity can grasp that which we are trying to show him.

To begin with, in making a drawing to scale, we must decide upon certain dimensions, but let it be understood that the dimensions shown on my drawings are for the purpose of illustrating only, as the type of window may vary considerably according to the size of the building. However, it is well know that in the construction of new buildings, standard sizes should be taken into consideration, such as glass sizes and lumber.

It will be noted that I have shown my wall of a height that enables me to use ten-foot studs, sawed in two, making the distance between plates five feet. The same thing should be taken into consideration when deciding upon the depth of a building, so as to use even lengthed material without waste. When laying out the window opening, we must first decide on how many lights we want our sash, the sash, of course, determining the width of the opening. After glass sizes have been decided upon, we then have the width of our opening and the distance from the floor to the sill, as it is necessary in this construction to have the sill the proper height from the floor to allow the sash to drop down. The sash is to be hinged on the bottom and the muslin frame at the top, allowing the frame to swing up and being held in place when open by a wire hook from ceiling or roof rafters.

When the sash or frame, or both, are closed, they are to be held in position with barrel bolts or steel buttons, this, of course, being done only when weather conditions are unfavorable.

In order to eliminate a ledge from snow or water to settle on, it is better to tack the muslin on the outside of the frame. which will form a smooth surface for the rain or condensation to run down onto the galvanized drip. The galvanized iron drip is important in the construction of this window, as it is for the purpose of carrying away all water that would otherwise follow the rabbet of the meeting rail and get inside the coop. Make a saw cut the full length of the bottom of the muslin frame to receive the edge or drip and tack or nail the face of drip to frame as shown in detail. Be sure to locate drip so it will not interfere with sash and frame when opening.

Should the size of this window be increased considerably, I would suggest making the sash and frame of heavier material to eliminate warping, and place a fastener in center to hold sash and frame together when closed. I would also use four hinges instead of three as shown. The entire opening is to be covered on the outside with wire netting tacked to the window frame.

Drinking Vessels for Fowls.

Too little care is given the fowls in providing them with clean, pure drinking water. All observing breeders of poultry have found that it pays to give the fowls only the best wholesome feed. They have noticed that the egg supply has increased materially after such treament; but many have forgotten that the principal part of the egg, as well as of the fowl itself is water. Pure fresh water then is of vital importance.

As a practical experiment, if you do not believe water plays an important part in the life and health of the fowl, try giving

the fowls tainted or stagnant water for a few days and notice how quickly the eggs become tainted and strong and unfit for use. Keep the water supply entirely away from the fowls for one whole day, and note how few eggs are gathered the next day. Reason how much better condition the fowls must be in by having plenty of cool water during the hot summer days, and water with the

Drinking vessel made from candy bucket.

chill taken off during freezing weather, by thinking of a really warm day last summer when you could not get a drink just for one hour.

There are many devices and fountains on the market, but the two illustrations given here show how the flock may be watered in a sanitary way for a trifle or no cost. The feature

shown about these methods of watering is that the devices are simple and neat and can be easily and speedily cleaned.

A candy bucket is cut down to the proper height in the one instance and a lid fastened to it by a couple of screen door hooks to keep the fow' from overturning it. Littl chicks cannot get in ar drown and the water is in t shade.

Drinking vessel made from cheese box.

In the other illustrati a cheese box is gotten from the grocery, the bottom remov and the slats arranged as shown in the sketch, and the rangement set over a gallon crock. You cannot imagine h convenient this fountain is until you try one.

The Sprouting Frame.

In the majority of suburban and village poultry yards it is an impossibility to have the poultry runs sodded down to grass or clover, as they are too small to permit this. The runs must be so large as to almost afford the fowls free range to keep them from destroying all the sod if the yards are sodded to begin

with. The lawn clippings make excellent green food during the spring and early summer, but somehow the fowls tire of them and they seem to become tough and unpalatable. You can make your bare poultry run produce fine succulent green food in a few days, provided it is not covered with cinders or

Wire top frame for growing green food for chicks and fowls.

ashes and is rich and fertile as poultry-runs generally are. Make a frame any desired length and width and about six or eight inches high, as shown in the illustration. Cover the top of it with one or one-half inch wire netting, being careful to get it on very tight, so it will hold up the weight of the fowls and not sag much. To keep the top from sagging much the frames should not be made over three feet wide. Spade up a plot the same size as your frame in the yard where the sun will shine most of the time. Pulverize the ground thoroly, as a quick growth depends upon this. Soak the oats twenty-four hours and after it is sown, rake it in thoroly. If it is watered regularly it will be scarcely no time until it is up and in the course of two or three weeks high enough that an occasional blade will grow thru the wire. The fowls cannot kill it while thus protected by the wire, but it will not grow above the wire you may be sure.

Breaking UP Broody Hens.

Owners of flocks of the Mediterranean class—Leghorns and Minorcas—will not be annoyed so much by the sitting hen, but all the heavier varieties in which the sitting instinct has not been bred out, attempt to sit after each clutch of eggs has been laid. Some of the meat breeds—the Brahmas, Cochins and the Langshans—insist so persistently in sitting that it is often

Tying a broody hen with string attached to leather band around the leg.

method is to make a yoke out out of a small forked sapling similar to the yoke used on fence breaking cattle. With this yoke about their neck the hen cannot remain on the nest with any degree of comfort, but she can manage to eat.

A hen that is very persistent in sitting may be tied out under a tree with a soft cord for two or three days where she cannot find anything to roost or sit upon except the ground. Care should be taken to use something soft to attach to the leg. A leather band, as shown in the illustration herewith is very satisfactory.

a hard matter to break them up even when confined in an empty crate or box.

There are several other ways of breaking up the sitting hen besides the ordinary method of cooping them up in a box. One unique

The "yoke" plan of breaking a hen of sitting.

Where there are a great many sitting hens to break up, double compartment fowl shipping coop hung from the roof

This coop breaks the hen of sitting and does it in a humane way and in a much shorter time than other methods.

a shed or from the limb of a tree in the poultry rand the broody hens confined in it, will break the up quicker than any other method. The broody h will often attempt to in the dark corner of ordinary stationary cra but as the hen mo about in the crate h from a wire it swi causing the hen to th —if such the hen can —more about keeping balance than of sit Water should be given broody hens, together a scant supply of during the two or days of their con ment.

The Richmond Hopper.

Recently while on a trip I met an old friend who in turn introduced me to a traveling man friend of his. It was but a few moments until the conversation drifted to chickens and I found the traveling man an enthusiastic fancier. It is an old axiom that goes something like this: "Every one has some redeeming quality," and I apply this to my everyday life with this version, "We can get valuable information and lessons from every one we meet and see." It depends much, tho, how you go about it to be benefited by everyone and it is as much of an art to be able to acquire knowledge than it is to impart knowledge.

On this trip the traveling man gave me an idea with a

rough sketch on the back of an envelope of a feed hopper that I have found since to be all that he, in his enthusiasm as embryo inventor, claimed for it. The great difference between the hopper and all others which I have ever seen or made is that it keeps the feed working to the front while the others keep shelving it back away from the fowls. The dimensions do not need to be given, as they are plain enough in inches in the profile diagram. Try one or two of these hoppers as an experiment, and see how admirably they work. You can probably find a box at the grocery which will just answer the purpose.

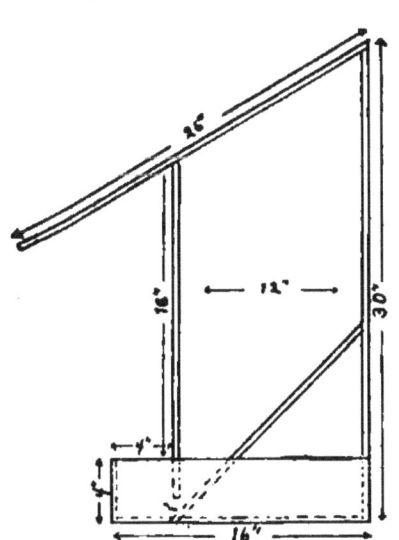

Caring for Eggs for Incubation.

To the average person raising poultry only as a side line on a few feet of back-yard on the back lot, it is hardly expedient to set hens before the first of April. The earth then will have had time to warm a little in our northern latitudes, before the chicks are hatched, and they will mature so much easier and faster under the later favorable conditions.

It is well, tho, to plan ahead and decide how many young chicks we intend to raise during the season and be thoroly prepared. To have fertile, strong eggs we must have vigorous parent stock, and to have chicks full of vitality we must have strong, fertile eggs. Much depends, too, on the care of the egg after it is laid and before it is placed under the hen.

Eggs for hatching can not be removed from the nest too carefully. They should not be placed in a large basket with a lot of other eggs. This often causes a very small crack, so minute that it can hardly be seen until the eggs have been under the hen several days and become soiled.

The hands that gather the eggs should be clean and free especially from any oily or greasy substance as the oil will surely enter the pores of the eggshell, thus smothering the germ. within. In going about from one nest to another and opening and closing doors we are most likely to jar the basket in which we are carrying the eggs, more than we realize, and enough to jar several germs from their web-like mooring between the yolk and white of the egg. During severe cold weather the egg should not remain in the nest until it becomes chilled or be removed from a warm nest out into an open basket and carried about in the cool breezes of the evening for several minutes while gathering eggs. It is more advisable to gather the eggs three or four times a day during cold weather. The shell of the egg should be observed from time to time and care taken that the fowls are supplied with oyster shell at all times if the eggshells are inclined to be thin and fragile. Eggs not well proportioned or with a rough surface should not be saved for setting and you should know whether your exceptionally good hen is laying a nice smooth egg.

Low, flat wooden trays or boxes make ideal receptacles in which to gather the eggs before setting them. The box should be lined with three or four thicknesses of newspaper, as paper is a nonconductor of heat and the eggs will not be affected by rapid changes in temperature so readily. It is much better to place one layer of eggs over the bottom of the tray, as then they can be easily turned each day. To turn the eggs, lay a row of them to one side and gently roll the rest over to their place and in this way the eggs will have been turned just half over, so that the part that was at the boottm the day before is now at the top. Paper makes a very good covering for the eggs, too. If they are left to the open air for ten days in a dwelling they will dry out more than were they left in a nest in the natural state built upon the moist earth. The temperature at which they are kept should be about 60 degrees Fahrenheit. Eggs of extraordinary fertility may be kept two weeks safely.

A Home Made Feed Hopper.

The hopper method of feeding poultry has proven one of the most successful devised during recent years. Many of the largest poultry plants, as well as the great army of back yard fanciers, are adopting it to the exclusion of all other systems.

It has been generally acknowledged that fowls thrive better when given free range and when they have an unlimited variety of food and can choose the morsels that happen to be appetizing at the time. Following this theory, poultrymen have attempted to provide their fowls with a complete variety of food and have it where they could get at it at all times. In attempting this the chief difficulty has been in keeping the food before them at all times without waste. The fowls persist in pulling the food out upon the ground whenever the feed box is so constructed that they cannot possibly do this.

The hen hopper has been an invitation to English sparrows and rats to make the poultry quarters their home. Cement floors and foundations will generally stop the rat nuisance, and if the feed hopper is placed in the poultry house sparrows will seldom bother it.

A very satisfactory hopper that will feed and not waste grain may be easily made from a soap box or small shoe box at a trifling cost.

The dimensions of the box shown in the illustration are not important, as far as height and width go, but the depth should invariably be from 11 to 12 inches. The hopper shown is made from an ordinary shoe box and is 12 inches deep and the same in width and about two feet high. This makes the hopper large enough to hold feed for a large flock.

After removing the side of the box which formed the lid, take out one end of the box. Place the lid in the position shown by the dotted line in the side view diagram, letting the bottom come to within four inches of the bottom and to about six inches from the front of the box. Take six inches of the piece that came out of the end of the box and tack it on in front at the bottom. This contrivance allows the feed to come down so it cannot clog and gives the space for the fowls to put their heads in and eat, but as the front is six inches high the birds cannot raise the feed over the front to waste it.

The lid of the hopper should be made quite slanting, so that the fowls cannot perch upon it. A piece should be tacked upon the back extending 8 or 10 inches above the back, to which a board wide enough to cover the top of the hopper is attached with leather hinges.

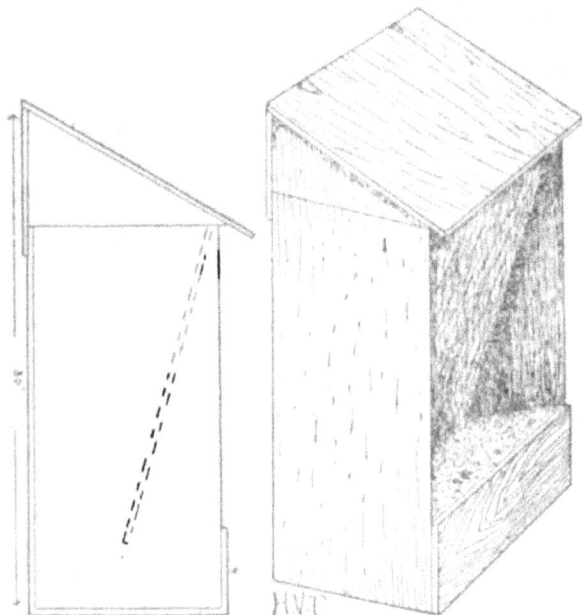

Feed hopper, made from a wooden shoe box.

The hoppers may be made in all sizes, from single ones six inches in width to three-compartment ones two to three feet in width, but all must be 11 to 12 inches deep from front to back to work properly.

One hopper should be provided for grit, one for bran, one for chop feed, one for beef scraps, and one, in fact, for all the different foods which should be before the fowls.

For the busy man with a small flock the hopper method of feeding the fowls is the solution to the vexing question how to get the fowls fed often enough and at the right time each day, especially during winter. Many men go to work early in the morning and do not return until late in the evening. In these hoppers feed can be placed to last two or three days, or even longer. The fowls are released from the house early in the morning and watered and a little grain scattered in the straw to keep them busy and the drinking vessel is filled. All that is necessary in the evening is to gather the eggs and lock the house.

Successfully Shipping Eggs for Incubation.

How the eggs are packed for shipment is quite an important factor. It is one of the most important, I have found, for eggs as a rule are fertile, and the buyer, as a rule has had experience in hatching eggs to some extent at least and therefore between two experienced men it is a question of handling between and how they are packed for the handling.

I am convinced the better the egg box the poorer receptacle

it is for shipping eggs for hatching. The expressmen of this country have learned by sight all the best egg boxes and know they will stand the weight of a man without breaking. They therefore throw them with impunity as they know they will land in the car, on the truck or platform, in good shape, as far as all outside appearances are concerned. Watch eggs being handled at some important transfer point in the busy season and you will agree with me. It used to be that eggs for hatching in boxes had to be handled with care but the manufacturers of boxes have so improved them that the average box could be dropped from the second story window without injuring the box or breaking the egg—but, alas, with the germ!

I like a good egg-box. No one admires a good box more than I and I believe they have their place, but from costly experience I have found it does not pay to intrust them openly to the expressman. Nothing beats a basket, I have found, and the place for the box is in a basket. A basket cannot be handled very roughly without being broken and the price of the eggs comes out of that particular expressman's pocket when the checking-up time comes. Eggs packed in a basket are not nearly as safe as when they are first packed in a box and then the box placed in a basket.

When eggs are packed separately in a basket, you will find each egg gets the benefit of the jar given the basket, but first pack the eggs in a box and the box in a basket, and the box of eggs is like a brick in a basket of straw. Shake the basket all you please, the box by its compact, heavy weight, juggles about like a cork on water, never once getting the benefit of a sudden or quick jolt.

I have seen people pack eggs in boxes with bran, sawdust, and what not. The eggs arrived unbroken but a poor hatch resulted, because every egg was packed in so firmly that every jar and jolt of the box was directly transmitted to the eggs just as the tap, tap, of the dentist's hammer is directly transmitted to your sensitive tooth thru the medium of a little chisel. The germ of the eggs is just as sensitive as your sore tooth.

Candy buckets, and other buckets I have also seen used. The eggs were packed in oats or bran or rice hulls and they were packed so well and the bucket was such a good bucket that the expressman knew he could handle it just about as he pleased without breaking the bucket and as long as the bucket did not break the eggs were safe. That is the wrong principle upon which to ship eggs. Pack them securely in a box so the eggs will be heavy and compact in the center. Then pack the box in a frail nickel market basket or bushel basket, as the case might be, packed in chaff or straw and covered over tightly with cloth. The package appears frail and this is the impression you must make with the expressman all along the line—but it is deceiving and not frail, because it puts the expressman on his guard with the result that the eggs arrive safely.

I have known instances where eggs in patented boxes, after three successive trials, could not be shipped thru three states so they would hatch, but when shipped as above directed had nine to hatch. I have known other cases, to my personal knowledge, where eggs were shipped a thousand miles and every egg hatched but one; another time all but two and cases like these are without number. In my case it has come to be that I can almost instantly tell whether eggs have been packed right at a glance, as there are only two ways—a right and wrong—and it is like thumping a watermelon to see if it is ripe, only it is much easier to tell if a shipment has been packed right or not.

If I were buying eggs for hatching I would not buy them unless they were packed on their sides, each egg wrapped and packed securely in a box and the box in a basket of straw or chaff. If the buyer of eggs would only consider, even if he had to pay 25 cents additional, that he was eliminating a vast amount of chance from the transaction, to have his eggs packed first in the best egg box obtainable and then in a basket.

I am convinced that eggs should not be shipped on end, Nature does not place them on end and it is an unnatural position and the web holding the germ is constantly on a strain in this position. This is often the cause of a poor hatch. The web holding the germ is strung from end to end and when the egg is placed on end the web becomes taut and is easily broken. Place the egg on its side and the germ rests in the web like a hammock. Plain, isn't it? Never thought of it that way before, though.

Coops for Hens and Chicks.

The hen expected to raise a large brood of chicks should be provided with the best quarters possible. The coop should admit plenty of sunshine, should be wind, water, and vermin proof. It should be cozy and dry and afford easy access to all parts for cleaning and caring for the little chicks. The floor should be near enough the ground that the little chicks after getting out can easily find their way back and yet far enough off of the surface of the ground to insure dryness and prevent the harboring of rats. The coop should not be cumbersome or elaborate, yet it is advisable to build it substantially.

The box shaped coop shown in the illustration is well adapted to the needs of the small fancier with only a few broods raise in his back yard, during the spring, or the large poult

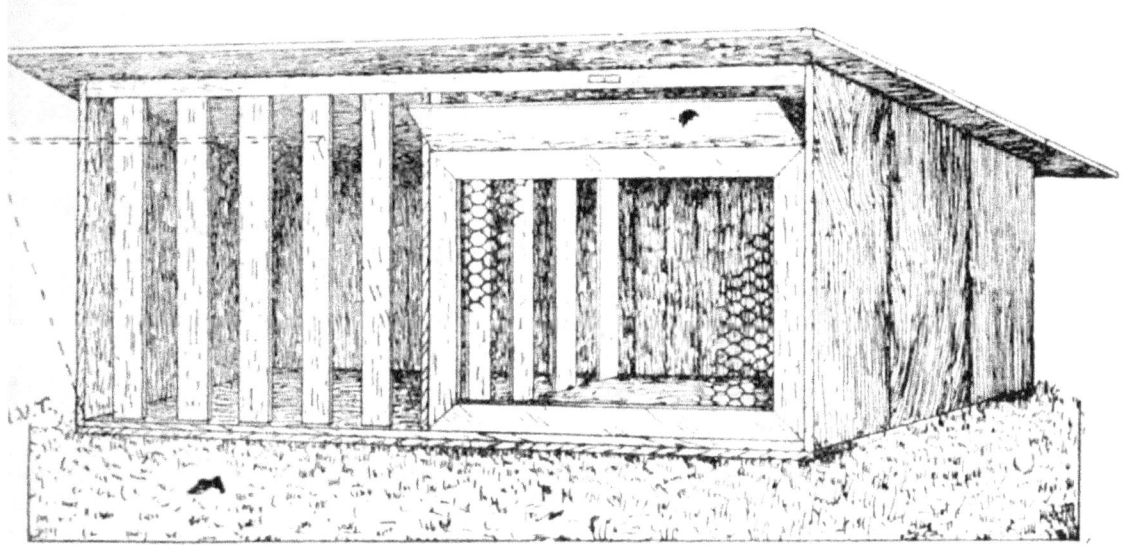

Coop for hen and chicks.

raiser who raises large number of chicks with hens. It is
built on the open colony type plan.

The coop is 36 inches long by 18 inches wide, and 18 inches
high in the rear and 24 inches high in front. It is divided into
two compartments, making each compartment 18 inches square.
Using these dimensions, even length lumber may be used with
scarcely any waste. The two side walls and back are made
tight fitting, and it is well to cover them with roofing paper,
if tongue and groove siding is not used. The roof should be
of light pine lumber covered with roofing material. Shingles

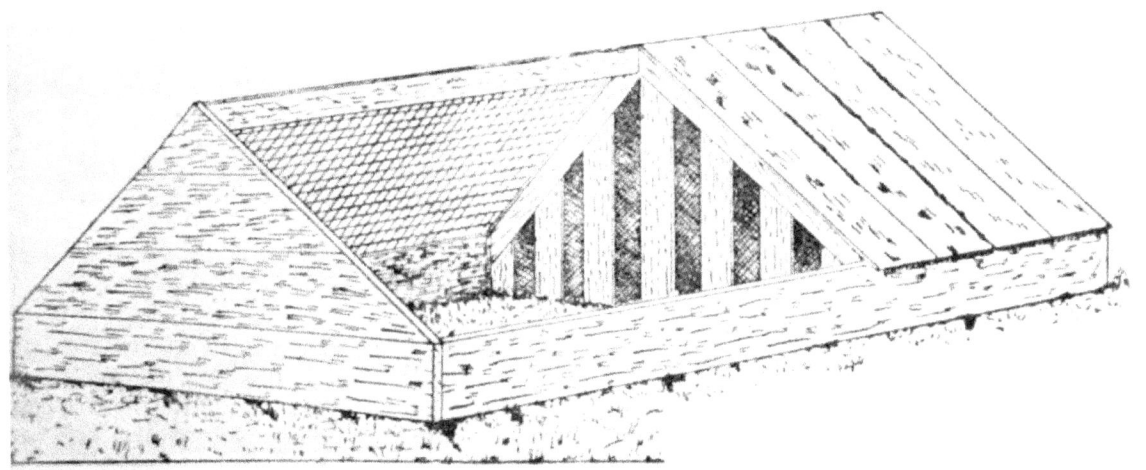

The modernized "A" coop.

are not adapted to this coop, or any coop or poultry house for that matter, as they require too steep an angle, thus requiring additional lumber, and, also, they harbor lice. All roofs for any kinds of poultry houses should be as flat as possible to hold the warmth down next to the fowls during the winter, and the same applies to cooping hens and chicks.

The compartment in which the hen is confined is to the left, and is divided from the one to the right by slats. The dotted lines represent the door, which is hinged at the bottom in front of this compartment, and acts as a platform in front of the coop during the day, and at night as a tight fitting door, excluding rain, wind, and rats alike. One or more of the slats in front should be made loose fitting, so the hen may be released.

The compartment to the right, or sun parlor, is fronted with a door covered with one-half inch mesh wire netting, which will exclude cats and weasels. A little trap door is made directly above the wire door, shown partly open in the illustration, and thru which the feed and water is given to the chicks early in the morning before the dew is off the grass and while they should yet be confined. The little fellows cannot slip past your hand when fed thru this door, as they do so often, to our great annoyance, when a door is opened near the floor thru which to feed them. In this sun parlor the chicks can be fed the small chick food and delicate morsels too expensive to fill the old hen's crop with. The little chicks can feed here early in the morning on rainy days, and when it is too cold to let them out, unmolested. The hen is fed whole corn at the same time, and cannot trample or bother the chicks. When the dew is off the grass, and the chicks old enough to be given the run, the door-platform in front of the hen's apartment is dropped to the ground, and the chicks get out into the open directly from the mother hen's compartment while the hen is confined. This makes a most admirable and convenient way for caring for the hen and her brood. For convenience, the floor may be made to drop out and the roof hinged.

The second illustration of a coop for hen and chicks is one of the old fashioned "A" coops modernized. The frame work in front is covered with one-inch wire netting, and in this par the chicks may be fed apart from the hen, and given a grass run.

The Setting of the Hen.

Many people who have been about chickens for years kno no more about setting a hen properly than they did when on tl farm these many years ago. They like to tell how mar chickens mother used to raise. But years soften their memo and they forget how many she did not raise and how many ju raised themselves and how many hens took this duty upon themselves and brought forth a brood in nature's way.

Again I cannot do better than to refer you to nature. The common domestic fowl is certainly a fowl belonging to the land. Not a bird of the air. So watch the common domestic hen in an isolated farming district pick out her nest, and invariably you will find she picks it upon the mother earth where there is straw and chaff with which to line the nest. You have noticed how the hen has that instinct sent down thru all these ages of throwing small straws up over her back and letting them slide down cozily about where they will. Occasionally a hen will take to the hay mow, but this does not prove the rule untrue that the hen is a land fowl. It only shows that she is bewildered by her long association with man in domestication and has not followed the dictates of nature.

I would like to have the eggs wasted each year through faulty nesting conditions. I would have enough to retire on I am sure. Instead of man giving the hen a natural position in a natural surrounding he is just as liable to make a nest in a deep excelsior box and have the hen jump down in the nest. What happens? The hen soon breaks an egg and after that it is only a question of a few days until the whole lot is ruined.

Many make the mistake of placing the eggs in a brand new nest. I have scruples against this plan. I like old nesting material that has been used by the laying hens. It seems more like nature would have it. A deep nest of new straw or any other material gives too much ventilation to the nest and accounts for many failures.

The best way to set a hen is to place the nest in a cheese ring or low box where the hen can walk directly onto the eggs without jumping down on them. During the early part of the spring it is well to have a bottom in the nest container, but after the middle of April in our latitude I knock out the bottoms and have the nest directly upon the ground in a nice secluded place where air and light can enter. Many times I scoop out a little hollow in the earth and have no box of any kind. The hen will attend to keeping every twig and straw within many inches around snugly in her nest. Set in this manner the hen will attend to business and seldom breaks an egg. I change hens about and never set the hens where they wanted to set in the first place. I give them the eggs at night and cover them over with a good roomy box and then do not bother them until the second day. The first three days are the most critical and you have over half of this time gone already. Watch that the hen gets back on her nest and you can cover her up again once or twice and by that time she will go back without any trouble. Too many people fuss and worry too much with their setting hens. First place them in a quiet secluded place.

Don't fool them with glass eggs, but place confidence in the hen and your judgment that she surely wants to set. Then give her a full set of eggs and cover her up and kept thus in the dark she will stick right to business, and as I said above, very shortly will go right back to her nest and no more trouble out of her until the chicks hatch.

The food the hen gets is important. Don't feed soft feeds. Feed hard grains only. There is nothing better than corn. Have plenty of grit and water before them, also a dust bath. Keep free of lice and with this kind of treatment where she can get a full feed of corn once a day unmolested, you will take the hen off the nest in good condition and with a full nest of chicks. Do not again make the mistake of setting the hens in a deep box or in too much new deep straw, but let the hen have some choice in the matter and you will fare better.

Drinking Fountain for Chicks.

It is important that the little chicks have plenty of pure fresh drinking water at all times. It is not always easy to provide it, however, especially when the chicks are supplied water

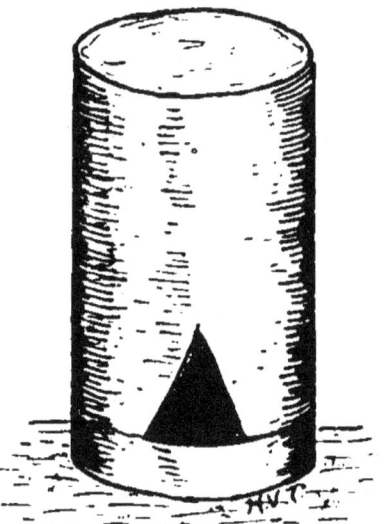

Tin can drinking fountain for fowls.

in the ordinary way—from a shallow saucer or tin pan. The saucer of clean water becomes dirt laden in a very few moments as the chickens play about in it. If filthy drinking water is allowed to remain before the chicks any length of time they will invariably fall a prey to some ailments to which they are subject while young.

Drinking vessels should be thoroly cleaned once a day and scalded at least once a week with a little soda added to the water. Galvanized tin or earthenware vessels are the best. The larger the vessel especially for adult fowls, the better—the water remains cool much longer. In warm weather the drinking vessel should be set in a cool, shady place and never where the direct rays of the sun fall upon it. The water in the little chicks' vessels should be changed four or five times a day and in that of the adult fowls at least twice a day during the summer months.

Instead of using an open saucer or pan for a watering ve

sel a water fountain can be provided at small cost. Gallon and
two-gallon containers are the best sizes for adult fowls. A very
satisfactory inverted fountain for the little chicks can be made

from a tomato can by
punching a few holes
around the edge of the
can near the top and
after filling it and in-
verting the saucer over
it, quickly turning it up
with the saucer under-
neath as shown in the
illustration.   Only   a
small amount of water
is in view at one time
and yet as it is used

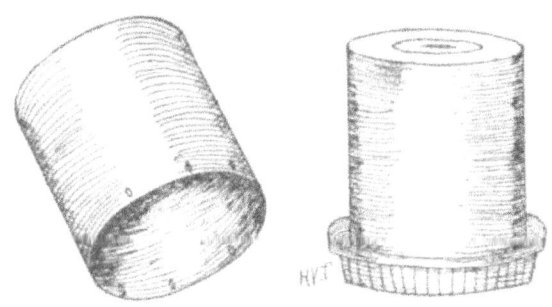

Drinking fountain for little chicks. Made
from tin cans as described in accompanying
article.

up the saucer is continuously refilled to the top of the holes in
the tin can.

Another very simple way of making a drinking fountain
for the little chicks which have a fondness for getting into the
water with their feet is by taking a pound baking powder can
with lid fitting down over the can and push a dent in one side
as shown in the illustration. The can is filled with water,
the lid placed over it and the can inverted.

Moisture and Ventilation in Incubators.

It is important that eggs placed in the incubator be incubated under conditions as nearly natural as possible.   The
fact that an incubator hatches a fair percentage of the chicks
from the eggs placed in the machine should not be taken as
evidence that the incubator is a great success and the equal of
the hen. Many incubators hatch the eggs but do it in an unnatural way and the chicks are weaklings and soon fall prey to
some disease and die. A fair percentage of the chicks hatched
in an incubator, even if they are improperly incubated, can be
raised to maturity if placed with hens, or the chicks may be
hatched under a hen and raised in the crudest kind of a brooder
and many of them will reach maturity. But if hatched in a
poor incubator and then a poor brooder, the task will be difficult
if not impossible.

Keeping the lamp well filled and clean and the wick trim-
med and the temperature at the proper degree will not always
insure a good hatch, although strong and fertile eggs are used.
The problem of getting sufficient ventilation and moisture is an
important factor and one that must be worked out entirely by

the operator. Evaporation goes on more rapidly in thin shelled eggs than in thick ones. The atmosphere absorbs more moisture in the summer than in the early spring and thus a machine that hatches well in the spring without being supplied with moisture will require some if it is operated in the late spring and summer. The machine that is ventilated with a sufficient amount of pure air will dry off the eggs much faster than the machine that is not ventilated so well. But neither machine will hatch properly without the right amount of ventilation and moisture. Possibly more machines make poor hatches for want of moisture than because of an over abundance of it.

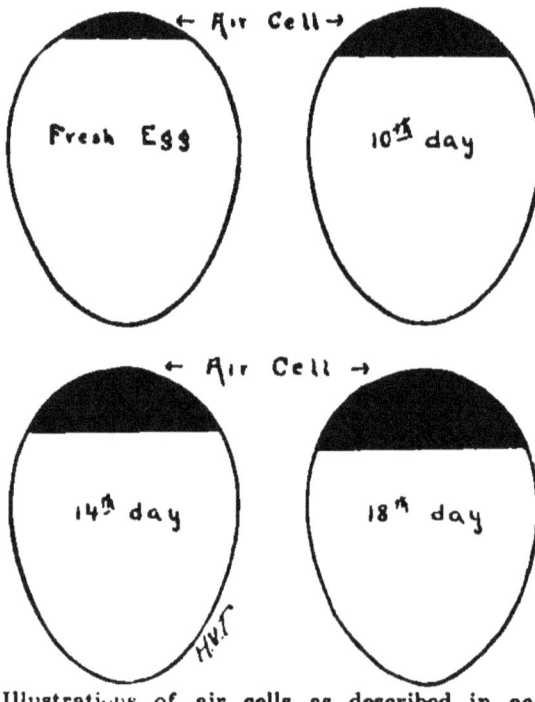

Illustrations of air cells as described in accompanying article.

If an egg, containing a live chick, be opened on the eighteenth day of incubation, the chick will be found to be full sized, but the yolk of the egg will be lying loosely, encircled by a netting of bloody vessels. During the last twelve hours before the chick breaks the shell, the yolk passes bodily into the chick. It is the chick's principal nourishment for the first two or three days of its life and is gradually absorbed. This is the reason chicks just hatched do not need food during the first forty-eight hours. In fact, food is not good for them during this time. When the eggs in the incubator are dried out too much during incubation, the yolk gives up a certain amount of moisture, with the result that it becomes waxy and cannot be readily assimilated by the chick which consequently dies in a few days. The non-absorption of the yolk makes the chick appear even larger than it should and this fact deceives many into thinking that the little fellows are so nice and large and therefore, healthy. Whenever the temperature of the incubator is permitted to rise above 10 Fahrenheit several degrees and remain any length of time or until the eggs are warmed thru to that temperature causing rapid evaporation, the same conditions arise as when there is a insufficient amount of moisture during the whole hatch.

With the evaporation of the egg through the pores in the shell the air cell in the large end of the egg becomes larger. The air cell in the egg may be easily seen by placing the egg at the end of a paper tube and looking thru it at a strong light. An egg set under a hen under natural conditions contains the approximate amount of air space during the different periods of the hatch indicated by the dark portion of the diagram. By testing several eggs an average can be taken and by consulting the diagram shown on this page, it can be determined whether the eggs have a proper amount of moisture or not. The air cell will seldom extend directly across the egg, but generally in a diagonal line. The egg should be turned over and over while being tested, to determine the full size of the air chamber.

Late hatches require moisture from the first day the eggs are in the incubator. There are several ways of applying moisture in the egg chamber. A flat pan, covering almost the entire floor under the egg tray, filled with sand and kept moist is a very satisfactory way. Two or three bricks which have been soaked in water will answer very well, or a damp cloth may be placed over the eggs. Warm water should always be used and the sand and bricks warmed before being placed in the machine. Otherwise the temperature will fall rapidly and remain low until the brick or sand has had time to warm. If the sand tray is used it may remain in the egg chamber during the whole hatch and warm water poured over whenever the sand dries. A hundred-egg machine will require several quarts of water during the progress of the hatch, and especially in dry weather and during the summer. The writer is waiting to see the machine that will hatch as strong and liveable chicks without moisture as the old hen which steals her nest out upon the ground in the grass or fence corner—all or many claims to the contrary.

Hatching Eggs in Incubators.

The incubator has long since passed out of the experimental stage, as far as practicability is concerned, and the incubator has so successfully vied with the hen as to almost deprive her of her favorite occupation. Nevertheless, all the incubator manufacturers are continually seeking to improve their machines so that, although we have not seen the perfect machine, some are almost so. Almost any of the numerous makes on the market today will produce fair results under favorable conditions.

The mechanism and heating and ventilating devices and appliances differ in each make of machine. The instructions sent out with each machine should be studied carefully, therefore, and, though you may have operated the machine a season or two before each hatch the instructions should be reread. If the instructions have been misplaced, don't fail to send for more before attempting to use it again. Many know so much about incubators in general and of every make that they think it useless waste of time to read the instructions and this is often the cause of a machine not working properly. The manufacturer is glad to co-operate with his customers to assist in getting the best results and a good name for his incubator.

A room for the location of the incubator should be selected in which a moderately even temperature can be maintained. A room containing a stove, as a rule, is not a suitable place, as it varies too much and is too warm. A room adjoining that containing the stove is better. It must be remembered, too, that stoves often emit fumes. These must be guarded against; so, also, must drafts be prevented.

The idea prevails that the cellar is the best place in which to operate the incubator, but the great majority of the cellars are wholly unfit for such purpose, especially at this time of the year. After the cellar has been aired several weeks and the atmosphere outside is warm, it may be safely used. At this time of the year have the incubator placed where there is plenty of fresh air and sunshine.

It is well to start the machine at least two days before the operator intends to place the eggs in it. Care must be taken not to fill the hot water machines too full at the first filling. Warm rain water should be used. The lamp in both the hot water and the hot air machines should be started low and gradually increased. The damper over the lamp should be raised just a little from the start to make draft for the flame and prevent smoking. Every half hour or so the regulator will have to be released a little more until the temperature reaches 100 degrees Fahrenheit. It will not have to be released to reach 103 degrees. The lamp bowl and burner cannot be kept too clean. If the lamp makes fumes at any time, it is because the bowl and burner are not clean. If the smallest amount of oil is left on any part of the lamp, the heat from the flame will soon cause the oil to evaporate or turn to a gas, and this is the odor we often detect where kerosene lamps are used and not kept scrupulously clean.

A new wick should be used for each hatch, and the charred part scraped off with a match or blunt stick each evening. Cutting with shears pinches the wick too much. Far more satisfactory results are obtained from the best grade of incubator oil. It makes a clean flame and burns without flickering. Never try to be so saving as to try to regulate the machine to such a fine point as to cause the damper to fit down tight, as the best oil and lamp will then smoke. Should the tank become covered with soot it should be wiped off and polished, or you will find it difficult to keep up the temperature. Soot is a nonconductor of heat.

The eggs should be placed in the tray with the small ends pointing downward and all in the same direction. Too much care can not be exercised in running the incubator the first four days. If the temperature goes up several degrees a poor hatch will result. If anything, run the machine low the first four days —102 degrees is high enough.

On the seventh day the eggs should be tested to discover the infertile ones. All clear ones should be removed and the doubtful ones marked and tested again two days later. After the fourth day the eggs should be turned twice a day, preferably with the hands. The eggs need not be turned until the end of the second day. See to it, however, that an even temperature is maintained.

On the fourteenth day the eggs may be again tested and all eggs that have a small black speck in them and seem dead should be removed. It is always best to remove the infertile eggs. Fresh eggs should not be placed in the bad eggs' places or eggs piled on top of one another to get more in the incubator. A hen or two can be set the same time the incubator is started and her eggs used to fill up the machine after the infertile eggs have been removed. The temperature should be kept as near 103 as possible after the fourth day.

Caring for Incubator Chicks.

The eggs in the incubator should be turned for the last time on the eighteenth day and the thermometer placed in a position where it will not be displaced by the hatching chicks. The ventilators should be opened as wide as possible and the temperature maintained at 103 degrees or a little above. As the hatch progresses it will be noticed that the lamp must be turned lower and lower each day and while the eggs are hatching scarcely any flame at all is required. This is caused by the chicks themselves supplying a great deal of heat.

White eggs will generally hatch a day earlier than the brown and fresh eggs hatch sooner than older ones. White eggs, if fresh, when placed in the incubator and the temperature kept a little high during the hatch will begin to pip on the eighteenth day. The hatch is not as successful, though, as when the eggs pip on the nineteenth or twentieth day. When the incubator has been allowed to cool off once or twice and the temperature during the hatch to fall below 103 degrees the eggs will not pip until the twenty-first day.

It is a most interesting sight to watch the hatch through the glass door of an incubator. The shell is pierced by the chick's bill near where the circumference of the egg is the greatest. Instead of a large crack appearing in the shell like when the shell is cracked from some outward force, a small hole is made by the bill and is seldom more than a quarter of an inch across. Through this small hole the chick obtains air in abundance and, after waiting and resting several minutes, during which time it has been growing stronger on the oxygen taken into its body, struggles a little within the shell and the egg probably shakes a little if not held fast by the surrounding eggs. As a result of the struggle the chick changes its position and its bill again comes in contact with unbroken shell and soon it has cracked away another portion of the shell, and so on it struggles in its spiral motion within its prison until it has made a wide hole all the way around the egg or nearly so, when, with a sudden display of strength, the cap of the egg, or cell, breaks away and the chick finds itself free. The little wet chick will struggle in a very frantic way for a moment and to those un-accustomed to the sight it may seem that the chick is a freak and will never gain control of its body. But, after lying still for another moment, it will suddenly open its mouth to obtain more air and then struggle again. After it has dried off thoroughly it will soon gain control of its legs and begin to walk about. Then, if at any time, is when the little fluffy ball is the prettiest. Should you weigh it and the shell from which it came you will find that it weighs somewhat less than the egg did when first placed in the incubator. This is because of the evaporation of the egg through the pores of the shell during incubation.

The incubator should never be opened while the chicks are hatching as the cold air striking the egg just broken or the little chick just out, chills it, and, in the one case the chick is so weakened that it never frees itself from the shell, and in the other the chick dies. Only in rare cases where the weather has been very dry and moisture has not been supplied in sufficient quantities to the incubator will the chicks need any assistance in breaking the shell. The chicks that are too weak to free themselves from the shell seldom live or make strong chicks if they do live, when helped out artificially.

After a chick is hatched the empty shell frequently lodges over an unhatched egg. If a visit is made to the incubator every half hour or so this can be easily prevented. In this case the door must of course be opened but it can be accomplished very speedily if you will try.

As the first three days the eggs are in the incubator are the most critical, so the first few days of the chick's life are the most critical. Too much caution cannot be used. In the great majority of cases many of the chicks die a week or two week after being hatched the cause was improper care the first three or four days.

There is no better place for the chicks the first two days than in the incubator itself. After removing the shells and placing the thermometer in the tray with the chicks and a piece of newspaper for a carpet on the tray, the incubator may be closed and the temperature gradually lowered to 90 degrees or a little above. The chicks need no further care until thirty-six hours after the last chick was hatched. They have a reserve of strength stored within that is sufficient for their need. In the natural state under the hen the eggs do not hatch at the same time and then the chick must develop enough strength within itself to hurdle from the nest and follow the hen several feet before the first bright crystal of sand or seed is found. The hen generally takes the new brood off the nest the first thing in the morning, too, so that it is not necessary to go very far before some bright dew drops on blades of grass attract the chick's attention and in this way it obtains its first drink of water. The incubator chick does not know what water is until it accidently falls into it or is taught by some one to dip its bill into the water. Therefore, it is well to dip each chick's bill into water on the morning they are placed in the brooder. Be sure, too, that each and every chick gets a drink.

The brooder should be running a day or more before the chicks are placed in it, so that it may be thoroughly warmed. It will not hurt the chicks to get out into the cold air for a few moments after the first two days, so they may be carried in an ordinary basket from the incubator to the brooder with an old cloth thrown over them. The old hen which stole her nest and hatched a brood is never in haste to leave the nest with her chicks, so don't be in a hurry to remove the chicks from the incubator. Have the floor under the hover covered with some sand and chaff. The chicks should be compelled to remain in the hover compartment the first day. A small tray of water placed in a light place and some fine grit and small seeds scattered about on the floor. Millet seed will do but the prepared chick feed is better. Some have poor luck with millet. Wet or moist mashes or feeds are considered by some to be not nearly so good as seeds but the little chick's system should not be overloaded with dry seeds.

The scratching apartment or sun parlor of the brooder should also be covered with a liberal supply of chaff from the haymow. After the first day in the brooder the chicks should always be fed in this part. Beef scraps and small tender blades of grass chopped fine should be fed at the end of the first week and also be in their diet after that time.

The best location for the brooder is on a plot of short grass near some fresh spaded earth where the chicks can scratch and find the minute forms of animal life which they relish so much. The earth should be freshened up every day by raking or spading it. This is why the edge of a corn patch or garden is such a fine place for chicks. Remember the chicks do not do as well on the fresh, bare earth alone, or on the sod alone. The combination is the thing.

After the first week the temperature in the brooder may be lowered to 85 degrees. On warm days the lamp may be turned out several hours during the middle of the day. The hover should always be warm at evening though, until the chicks feather out. The mistake is made too often in having a cold brooder. Take example from the old hen and you will notice she never changes her temperature much and the chicks run to her many times during the nicest days, while yet young, to get warmed up and these repeated warmings is what makes them grow fast and be able to ward off diseases that brooder chicks often fall prey to.

Advantages of Marking Chicks.

Those who have been rearing high class fowls any length of time have already learned how to mark their chicks so as to identify them when grown, but there are many, perhaps, who are hatching thoroughbreds from different pens for the first time and contemplate line breeding. Marking has a number of

Method of Marking Chicks Feet

advantages. No matter if the neighbor has the same variety of fowls, when the web in the little chick's feet is punched with a small poultry punch made especially for the purpose, the birds can be identified by the mark and the combination used. Moreover, to breed intelligently it is absolutely necessary that the chicks be marked, the progeny of each mating receiving a destinctive marking. In mating up the pen another season this will be a safeguard against inbreeding as it is possible by this method to know what relation, if any, the fowls bear to one another. Again, by marking the chicks from the different matings, we can know which mating produced the best chicks and can mate accordingly next season. In buying eggs from another breeder, also, it is always desirable to know what kind of mature fowls the eg produce, and it is impossible to know this unless the chicks are marked. The marks serve also to establish the age of the fowls from year to year.

The accompanying illustration shows how the chicks may be marked in sixteen different ways—the limit of the combinations because there are only four webs in the two feet and four squared is sixteen. Each pair of feet is numbered. The holes are punched in the small web between the toes of the chick. It is practically a painless operation, and the chicks seem scarcely to notice it if punched the first few hours after hatching. The fowls, as a rule, carry the mark as long as they live. Care should be taken not to place the hole too near the outer edge of the web, or it will tear out. As each brood is hatched, carefully mark each chick, using a different arrangement for each pen of eggs represented, changing the arrangement in a manner similar to that indicated by the dots in the illustration.

Have a blank book in which to record the marks and, as the chicks are marked, record them by marking a diagram of the dots as they appear in the web of the feet. Opposite the diagram record the pen or breeding from which the eggs were obtained, the date of the hatch and any other information that may be of use in the future.

A Fireless Brooder.

Only during the late spring and summer it is advisable to attempt to brood chicks artificially without heat. Some forty years ago the theory was first advanced that chicks could be brooded artifically by confining the heat made by the little chicks' bodies, but not until quite recently has this theory received general attention. The assertion has been made that chicks could be brooded by this method out of doors during the most severe winter weather, and some who have tried it have been successful. The process has hardly left the experimental stage far enough, however, and the attempt to use it on a large scale should not be made until it has been tried on a small scale first.

But the fireless brooder may be employed for secondary use for brooding in warm weather or in heated houses. It may be also used in emergency cases where the hen leaves the brood a little too soon, when the brooder becomes overcrowded, or when the brooder is wanted for another and younger flock, but where it is hardly time for the brood to take to the colony houses.

The principal object sought in building one of these brooders is to make all parts easily accessible for cleaning and for caring for the chicks, to confine the heat as much as possible and yet have a good supply of pure air, to have the hover adjustable and padded with plenty of heatholding cloth, so the chicks may have something to press their backs up against as they do when brooded by the hen.

The brooder shown in the illustration is made in four different parts, each of which may be easily and quickly cleaned. The outside measurement of the box is 2x2½ feet and the height is eight inches. The floor is made to fit up in the box so that the four walls fit tightly on the floor of the brooder house. Where the walls of the box sit on the floor of the brooder it is too easily displaced and does not fit tight enough. Four holes are made in the corners of the box an inch apart and the top hole an inch from the top ledge of the wall. A peg fitted into one of the holes in each corner holds the hover at any height suited to the age of the chicks. There are also four large holes in the walls of the box, one on each corner an inch or an inch and a half in diameter for ventilation.

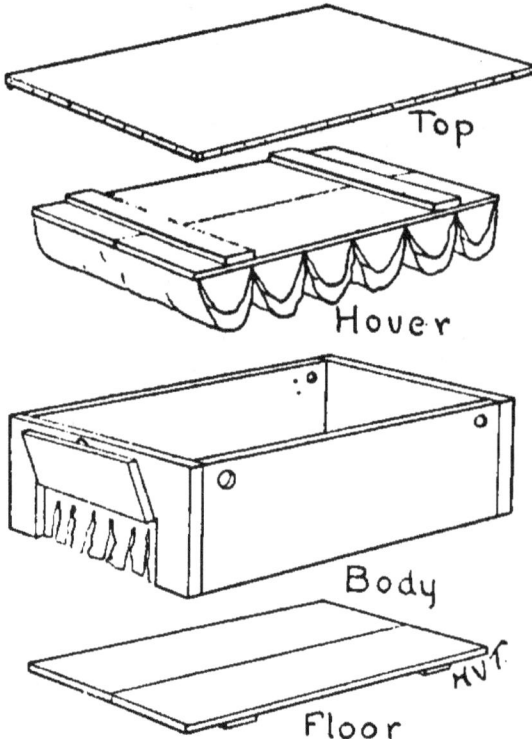

Drawings of the parts for the fireless brooder.

These ventilators are made big enough so that the air must pass through the cloth of the hover before it can reach the chicks. In this way there is a continuous inflow of pure air without a draft. Tin slides may be made to fit over the ventilators so the supply of air may be regulated during exceedingly cold nights.

The hover shows two folds of cloth dropped down, but another fold or two may be added with good results. The cloth is dropped, too, in folds without being cut into long strips as is the usual case and this makes the retention of heat much easier. Woolen flannel is the best material to use. An old blanket is generally available. The top is made to fit down tightly on the box and may be roofed with tarred paper or tin if it is to be used outside during the summer. The brooder should not be used, though, out in the open, but a good smooth roof is provided more as a roosting board than anything else as the chicks soon take to it after they feather out well.

Feeding for Quick Growth.

Those who wish to use a modified system of the hopper feeding plan may use troughs like the illustration for this purpose. The feed for the fowls for the day is placed in a divided trough, mash in one end and mixed grain or cracked corn in the other. The daily allowance of the food so fed varies

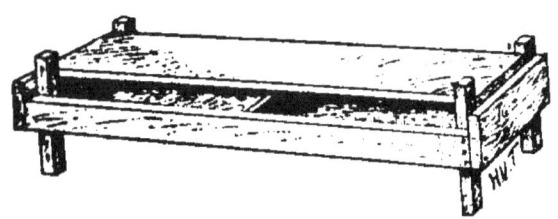

a little according to the season and the appetites of the birds.

The daily allowance for twenty-five fowls supplied in this trough should be a little less than three pints of moist mash and about

Home made feed trough that does not waste the food.

2½ quarts of dry grain mixture. The birds should be fed rather liberally, as there is no profit made with fowls fed on a scant ration. Just enough should be fed tho so that there is rarely any feed left in the trough at night.

This method of feeding is especially well adapted to the needs of the large poultry farmers where the main object is to make the youngsters grow to a marketable age as quickly as possible and with the least attention. Then where egg farming is carried on and the hens are kept out over the fields and grouped in colonies of 35 to 50 this is an ideal way, supplying them with plenty of food without making the feeding place a drawing card for rats during the night, as the fowls clean the feed up before night. When the trip is made around the farm with a one-horse wagon in the morning to feed and water, the attendant can keep in touch with the entrie flock, as they will not go out to range until they have been fed.

In the Little Compton district in southeastern Rhode Island where the Rhode Island Red was originated and made famous for this reason, the poultry farms generally use the trough system. This section of Rhode Island is noted for the great numbers of chickens raised and the practical poultrymen. Here men make the rearing of poultry a life study and make it a specialty just as sheep and cattle raising is made a specialty in many sections. The "one-man plants," as they are called, clear from $1,000 to $1,500 per year on their forty and fifty acre farms by egg farming and broiler raising. The product of these farms is shipped to Boston, Providence and New York principally. The Rhode Island Red fowl was originated by these farmers by a process of selecting the fowls each year which were best suited to their practical needs as egg layers and market fowls as well. This accounts for the widespread popularity of the Reds.

The daily mash fed on these plants varies some according to the season but generally consists of about half and half bran and chop feed (cracked corn and oats ground together) cooked until the corn is thoroughly done and then about ten or twelve per cent beef scrap added before feeding. During the winter cut steamed clover is mixed with the mash in about equal quantities.

The mixed grain is usually a mixture of cracked corn, whole corn, wheat and oats, the mixture being about 50 per cent corn in the summer season and a considerably large percentage during the winter season. After the chicks are old enough to eat mash they are fed the same feed as the adult stock as much time is saved which it would otherwise take in preparing additional food. Fish waste is fed quite extensively on these poultry farms in the spring to supplement the high priced beef scraps. Fresh fish waste can generally be obtained for twenty-five cents a barrel. The fish waste is well cooked before it it is fed and care taken not to feed too much to the laying stock as the fish taints the eggs. It is fed in abundance to the growing stock tho.

When one man cares for from 2,000 to 4,000 fowls each day the farm must necessarily be laid off to the best possible advantage that all the fields may be easily and quickly reached and the feeding done with expedience. All feeding and water appliances must be simple, easily used and cleaned.

The feeding troughs vary in size, but on an average are three and a half feet long by fourteen inches wide. Four upright posts on one-inch square stuff twelve inches long form the corner and legs. The bottom of the trough is made of a smooth board notched at the corners to receive the posts which serve as a frame as well as legs. The bottom board is nailed to the posts about four inches from the lower ends. On each side is nailed a piece three inches wide by three and a half feet long, giving a depth of about two inches to the trough. On each end is nailed a piece of board six inches high and fourteen inches wide which serves to form the end of the trough and support the removable top board. The top board or cover is of heavy inch stuff ten inches long, so that it will form a movable cover that is not easily shaken or jarred out of position. The whole makes a practical feeding device which keeps the food clean and prevents waste. There is little more than a three-inch clear open space for the feeding fowls between the top of the sides of the trough and the cover or lid.

Missouri Colony Brooder House.

By T. S. TOWNSLEY

Stove brooders afford the easiest and cheapest method of brooding large flocks of chicks. Farm poultry keepers who appreciate efficient equipment are rapidly discarding all other brooding methods in favor of the colony stoves. With the coal or oil heated colony hovers from three hundred to five hundred chicks can be handled in one flock with no more labor than is required with a few dozen chicks brooded with hens or in lamp heated brooders. The chick mortality is remarkably low on farms using colony stoves and little difficulty is experienced in raising early-hatched chicks. The fuel cost for brooders is low, and the stoves are durable.

Brooder stoves are used in all kinds of buildings, but best results are secured with a specially designed colony house. The brooder house should be ward, dry, well lighted and ventilated, and be large enough to furnish room for exercise. It should also be movable so that the chicks may have fresh groudn for their range.

The Missouri colony brooder house is designed to meet at least expense all the requirements of a farm brooder house. This house is built eight feet wide and ten feet long, with a gable roof. The gable roof construction has several advantages over other types. It requires less lumber, is more substantial, easier to move, and affords bet-

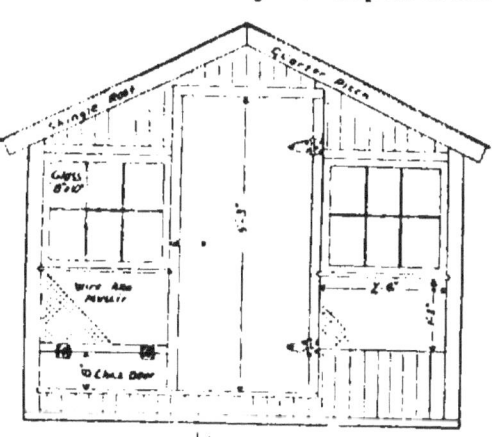

Front View.

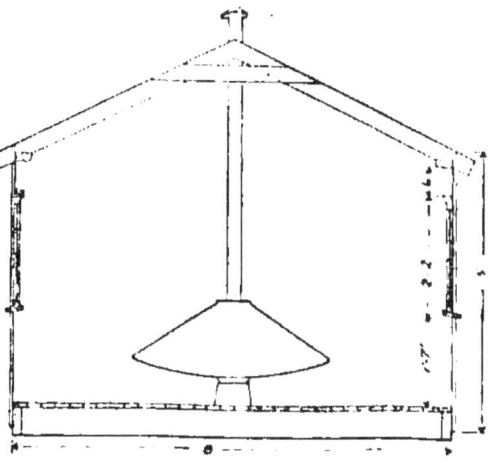

Cross Section.

ter interior arrangement than other houses.

.... **Building Details.**

Walls — T h e walls are of car siding, nailed up and down. This forms a tight wall and eliminates the use of studding except at the corners. Flooring may be used for walls instead of car siding. These tongue-and-groove materials make a tighter wall than other forms of siding and are no more expensive.

Floor—Ii a movable house a board floor is the only practical type. This floor should consist of a single layer of carefully laid matched flooring. A double floor is a needless expense.

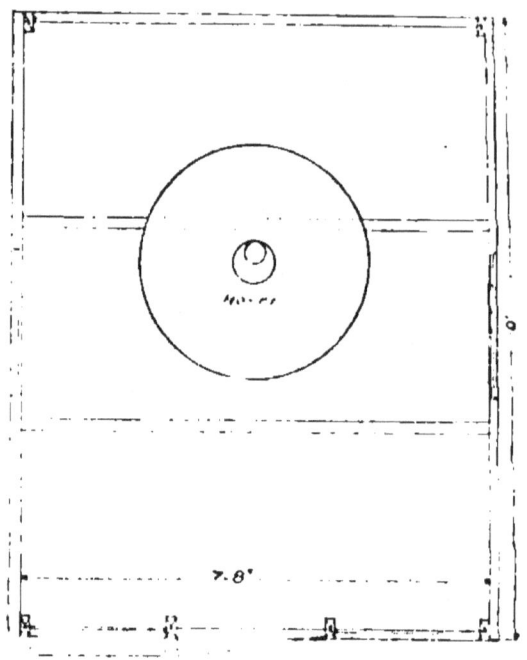

Floor Plan.

Roof—A shingle roof makes less weight on the building than most other types, and is less likely to be damaged in moving the house.

Foundation—A block under each corner of the house provides a satisfactory foundation. When the house is to be moved it can be set on a pair of skids.

Ventilation—Ventilation is secured through two openings in the south end of the house. These may be covered with muslin in stormy weather. Additional ventilation may be secured in warm weather by opening the windows.

Light—Four small windows supply light for this house. Two of these are placed in the south front and one in the east and one in the west sides. This arrangement insures good light in all parts of the house.

Cost of House.

The material in this house at current prices in Columbia will cost about $50. The cost of labor in building it should not exceed $10. In many sections of the state these figures can be considerably reduced.

The cost of a house of this type is not prohibitive for poultry keepers when the many uses which can be made of it are considered. After the brooding season is past the house makes ideal summer quarters for growing pullets. During the fall and winter months it will comfortably house twenty to twenty-five laying hens, or it will make a convenient house for storing feed. Before brooding time in the spring it can be used as a house for the breeding flock. The fact that it is easily moved adds very greatly to its usefulness.

Sill—Four pieces, 2x6—8; 32 board feet.
Sills—Two pieces 2x6—10; 20 board feet.
Rafters—Eight pieces 2x4—5; 27 board feet.
Plates—Two pieces 2x4—10; 13 board feet.
Studs—Four pieces 2x4—5; 13 board feet.
Door Posts—Two pieces 4x2—6; 8 board feet.
Nailer—Rear Wall—One piece 2x4—8; 5 board feet.
Short Pieces—Front—Five pieces 2x4—2½; 9 board feet.
Sheeting—Eighteen pieces 1x4—11; 66 board feet.
Finishing—Cornice—Four pieces 1x4—5; 7 board feet.
Finishing—Corner Strips—Four pieces 1x4—5; 7 board feet.
Finishing—Short Pieces—Four pieces 1x2—2½; 2 board feet.
Window Sills—Four pieces 1x2—2½; 3 board feet.
Finishing—Door—Two pieces 1x2—5½; 2 board feet.
Door Sill—One piece 1x3—5¼; 1 board foot.
Flooring—Thirty-two pieces 1x4—10; 107 board feet.
Siding—1x4, 225 board feet.
Total Lumber—547 board feet.
—Shingles One and one-quarter thousand.
Windows—Four six-light, 8x10 sash.
Wire Netting—For windows and open front, 15 linear feet of 2-foot wire.
Muslin—For open front, 1 yard.
Hinges for Door—One light pair and one heavy pair.
Hasp for Door—One 6-inch hasp.

Hatching Chicks and Their Color.

Because you have paid a good price for a setting of eggs from some breeder is no reason why you should apply the egg standard to the eggs you received and write saucy letters to the breeder because the eggs were not of the same shade or color. If he had known this was what you wanted he would have picked out the eggs at the corner grocery. Varieties laying tinted or brown eggs may lay many different shades of eggs. Some white egg varieties often have an occasional bird laying a tinted egg. Strange to say, these tinted eggs in the white varieties though if they hatch pullets, the pullets do seldom lay tinted eggs. They occasionally crop out when there is no occasion for it.

Therefore do not judge the chicks by the eggs. I once saw a setting of eggs from one of the most prominent breeders in the east which c st the buyer more than $1 each and among them was a very ill shaped egg. The egg hatched tho and this very chick turned out to be the very best in the whole lot.

The point I am making is that it only takes one egg to hatch the coveted first prize winner and it is all a matter of chance what color or shaped egg this chick will be hatched from. Leading breeders therefore do not like to take chances in eating a slightly ill shaped egg for they may be eating the golden egg.

Others get disappointed when after paying a fancy price for a setting of eggs to find that they get only a half dozen or say two or three chicks from the whole lot. Then they commence to figure that the chick or two cost them $5 or $10 or $15 each, as the case may be. But do not complain if you got one chick as far as blaming the breeder is concerned. Take pains and raise the one chick. It may be worth a whole flock. Nearly every breeder has a fertility guarantee and when eggs do not prove fertile take advantage of the guarantee. Many breeders also guarantee a certain number to hatch or replace at half price or some such arrangement. Therefore, if at first you do not succeed, try, try again. Do not grow suspicious of the breeder until you have given him a fair chance to live up to his guarantee.

Then again many keep their hopes and expectations at a high pitch until the eggs really hatch and then let them fall to earth because the chicks do not happen to be a certain shade or color. Remember again that is is just as hard to judge the mature fowl by the chicks, as it is to judge it by the egg.

All black fowls may be said to be black but all chicks hatched from eggs from black fowls are not black nor are they alike. The same may be said of the white fowls. Not only does the variety have a great deal to do with the color of the chick when hatched but different strains of the same variety often show a difference so pronounced that the experienced eye can note the difference.

Dispell then your fear for the next few weeks and withhold your judgment, if you have a bunch of chicks on hand from eggs you purchased. Because they do not look like the chicks from your own fowls of the same variety is no sign they will not turn out even better than your own stock|

Most people are sufficiently informed about chicks to know that Barred Rock chicks are not hatched with bars and yet I have known customers to call the breeder all kinds of names, intimating that he was crooked, because the chicks did not hatch with bars. This spring I heard of a case where a party paid $5 for a setting of eggs and then after he received them refused to set them and wired to the breeder at his expense asking for a return of his money because the eggs did not suit him in shape. When the breeder wired back the charges were reversed on him costing him 91 cents more and yet the buyer refused to set the eggs.

These are cases where "ignorance is bliss and to be wise is folly" is certainly not true.

The parti-colored or black red varieties, Brown Leghorns and Cornish chicks are very beautiful when hatched. There is a band or stripe of brown from the head to the tail and with lighter and narrower stripes on either side on the back. Over the rest of the body they are light brown or fawn. Brown Leghorns which are double mated can usually be told at hatching in that the light or female line chicks are very much lighter than the dark or exhibition male chicks. The male line are often so dark that the stripes blend on the back.

A black chick should not be hatched entirely black, if it is to be a green metallic black when grown. Some white shows good breeding. White about the head and breast in black chicks are the most satisfactory markings.

White fowls with yellow shanks should produce various degrees of creaminess or faint lemon yellow. A blue grey tinge to the fluff in white chicks will produce a white quilled chick invariably. But if a white chick from a white-plumaged and legged fowl has bluish shanks that thing, never clears. In fact, blue shanks on chicks, no matter what variety of yellow or white legged fowls, never clear.

The chicks from buff fowls come either with a yellow or buff cast, and have reddish-yellow legs. which gradually turn to white. The red is the blood showing thru the skin while after the scales on the leg form they do not permit the red blood to show thru.

Red varieties are very near like the buff, but they generally have shown more white and have a patch of brown on the back.

Black chicks always grow some white feathers in flights of

wings. Parti-colored varieties often do. This should not alarm you in the least. Parti-colored varieties should not necessarily grow white feathers at first, but it all depends upon the strain and care of the chicks. Chicks hatched in incubators and raised in brooders generally grow white feathers at first and time and again. I have seen chicks hatched from the same eggs and at the same time under hens and cared for in the natural way never develop the white in wings. Then again chicks confined while growing will often develop white no matter how they are fed or cared for.

The white chick developing and getting a black feather or two here and there will quite likely be your whitest adult so do not berate the breeder for selling you mongrel eggs.

Again chicks are often condemned because the legs are not yellow and should be so. Do not get excited. The chicks that have yellow legs at hatching time will fade while the chicks with darker legs, but with good yellow under foot, will produce the best yellow shanks.

To gain an advantage in mating up your pens for better results watch your chicks develop very carefully and you will soon find certain marks are marks of quality, while others are sure signs of being a cull. Experienced breeders can commence culling just as soon as the chicks are old enough for friers, but the beginner should not take this risk until he is thoroly familiar with the life history of the chicks of his variety else he may chop the head off his best bird unknowingly.

The Half-Way Coop.

After the hen has left her brood it is always a vexing question to know what to do with the youngsters. The coop that held them, and the hen beside, very comfortable a few weeks ago, is now much too small. The chicks are too small yet to attempt to teach them to take to the poultry house with the older fowls, and if the attempt were made the adult fowls would make life unbearable for them. The desire to go on the perch should be cultivated as soon, though, as the desire is shown. A large dry goods box roofed, as illustrated, makes an ideal half-way coop. The slats are placed close enough together so that the older fowls cannot bother the youngsters as they go to roost. The

The dry goods box coop suitable for the growing chicks.

small coop that they have been reared in thus far should be removed and this coop placed in its place. No matter how hard the storm, the rain cannot beat in with the wide extension roof, and yet the fowls are made accustomed to an open front house and plenty of pure fresh air. Take care that the young half grown fowls do not crowd together in a corner at night. This instinct is still in them to huddle up to something, although they really do not need the heat. If many are together in a flock they will crowd together very close and sweat. Along in the morning as it gets cooler they cool off too rapidly and fowls with a cold and roup is the result. It is far better to have them take to the roost, as they are sure not to crowd there. A one by three- or four-inch board laid flat makes an ideal roost for youngsters and will not produce crooked breast bones.

The Sun and Rain Shed.

Because of sudden showers, many little chicks become drenched and drowned during the early spring and summer because they could not get to a place of shelter soon enough or because they ran to the wrong coop in their excitement and the strange old hen kept them out until it was too late. Often the door to the coop blows shut or the opening is not large enough for all the little fellows to get in at once. For this reason there should always be provided handy an open place where the hen and chicks can get under easily in case of a sudden shower. A shed roof protection may be easily made out of a few old boards like the illustration, and it will come in handy many

A practical, easily made sun shade and rain shed.

times during the summer and save much worrying and annoyance about whether the chicks are all in out of the rain, when you happen to be away from home when the sudden shower comes up. You can make this frame most any size, according to your needs, but the more commodious the better. When several hundred chicks are raised several should be provided a convenient places and where the chicks range most. The stakes to which they are attached should be driven well into the ground and the shelter securely nailed to it so there is no danger of the wind collapsing it and killing the chicks.

It will be surprising to you to note how the fowls enjoy

the shade under the platform. Make the shelter quite near the ground and just so the fowls can barely stand under it, in preference to any other shade, during the very hot portion of the day. Burlap curtains hung from the sides make it more inviting and cooler.

An Ideal Colony House for Chicks.

To raise chicks in large numbers and yet have them strong and vigorous the colony house is almost indispensable. The largest and most successful poultry farms in the United States almost to a unit use the colony house in some form or other. The chicks can be housed in large brooders when young with good success, but when they are old enough to run about much

Colony house described in accompanying article.

they must have the advantage of more range than is afforded around a large brooder house where there are hundreds of other chicks the same size and age after the same bug and worm. Raising chicks to maturity in large flocks is like raising children in the heart of a large city. There is too much jostling about and too much excitement and too many after the same mouthful of food. Chicks must be raised like nature would have them, to be robust, strong and vigorous. Nature did not intend that two broods of chicks be cared for together, let alone several incubators full. Fifty little chicks are enough to have in one bunch after they get old enough to scramble about much.

The illustration of the colony house shown here is the one

that has been found most successful on the Fishel White Rock Farm. A batch of young chicks is placed in the house, which is provided with a brooder stove or hover attachment. The upper trap window is left closed during cold weather and the lamp under the hovers keeps the house amply warm. No matter how stormy or blustery the weather may be, the little fellows have plenty of dry floor space covered with chaff in which to exercise. Just the moment the sun comes out the two low windows in front give them the full benefit of it just where it is needed—on the floor in front.

The colony houses are generally kept up pretty close about the other buildings while the chicks are young, but just as soon as the clover fields commence to green out and fairly good weather is assured, they are moved out a little distance. As they grow older the houses are moved farther and farther until all the clover fields on the farm are occupied. The houses are moved as far apart as possible and rarely are they closer than three hundred feet in the row, and the rows are much farther apart. The houses are placed in rows and closer one way than another, so the attendant and wagon with water may reach them with as little driving over the field as possible.

After the chicks are weaned from the hover, roosts are put in the places provided for them, and the chicks take to them like old hens. Altho the chicks from the different houses wander together during the day they are never bunched together, and the fowls belonging to each house always gather about their own coop when feeding time comes. The houses are cleaned each morning with as much regularity as feeding is done. The roosts are painted with lice killer two or three times a week and thus lice and mites never get a start, and it is hardly ever necessary to pick up an individual bird and administer louse killer. Birds grown thus, as nature would have them, grow like weeds and they are a pleasure and delight to care for and attend to. Money in poultry! Of course there is when cared for like this.

The houses, as a rule, are about six by eight feet and six feet high in front and four or five in the rear. They are built on good stout skids so they may be dragged about over the place at will. A single good horse can handle them.

Planning the Spring Work—What to Do and When to Do It.

After the severe weather during the greater part of February, when many of our hens refused to lay, in spite of coaxing, we find it an easy matter to obtain eggs in March, which usually brings us comparatively mild weather. Unless you spend a great deal of time with the fowls you can hardly realize to what a great extent the tender blades of growing grass and minute forms of animal life enter into the hen's diet at this time of the year. This is really the secret of the increase in egg production—a fact readily proved when a few days of cold weather checks growth again. Of course we must be prepared for this, and supply the food the fowl can not obtain under such conditions. Even at this time possibly some are finding it difficult to get eggs in any great number, but it is because the fowls are confined in small, bare runs and improperly cared for.

It is interesting to note how we unconsciously catch the spirit of spring and before we are aware of the fact have our plans laid out to set so many hens during the next few days, or to start the incubator. But we must not forget that to have too may March chicks would cause more expense to raise them than later and necessitates much more care and fondling. This is not true of the poultry man who makes the raising of broilers and early fries a business, and is prepared for the early business, and is prepared for the early chick, but, to the average person who raises poultry only as a side line on a few feet of yard on the back lot, it is hardly expedient to set hens before the first of April. The earth then will have had time to warm a little before the chicks are hatched, and they will mature so much easier and faster under the later favorable conditions.

It is well, though, to plan ahead and decide how many young chicks we intend to raise and to be thoroughly prepared. To have fertile, strong eggs we must have vigorous parent stock and to have chicks full of vitality we must have strong, fertile eggs. Much depends, too, on the care of the egg after it is laid and before it is placed under the hen.

Eggs for hatching can not be removed from the nest too carefully. They should not be placed in a large basket with many other eggs. This often causes a very small crack so minute that it can hardly be seen until the eggs have been under the hen several days and become a little soiled. The hands that gather the eggs should be clean and especially free from oily or greasy substances of any kind as the oil will surely enter the pores of the egg shell and seal them up so the chick will be deprived of air and die in the early stages of its development. In going about from one nest to another and opening and closing doors we are most likely to jar the basket or bucket in which we are carrying the eggs more than we realize, and enough to jar several germs from the web-like mooring between the yolk and white of the egg. During the severe cold weather the egg should not remain in the nest until it becomes chilled or be removed from a warm nest out into an open basket and carried about in the cold breezes of the evening for half an hour or more while gathering eggs. It is more advisable to gather the eggs three or four times a day during cold weather if they are to be used for incubation. If two or more pens are mated and if it is from these that you intend to save eggs for hatching, a lead pencil should be carried along while gathering eggs and the egg marked with the date and the pen number as it is removed from the nest. Experts find this the only safe way to mark eggs, as many eggs are handled day after day and a mistake is sure to be made some time during the breeding season in marking if we wait until we arrive at the house. The shell of the egg should be observed from time to time and care taken that the fowls are supplied with oyster shell at all times if the egg shells are inclined in the least to be thin and fragile. Eggs not well proportioned or with a rough surface should not be saved and you should note whether your exceptionally good hen is laying nice smooth eggs.

Low, flat wooden trays or boxes make ideal receptacles in which to keep the eggs before setting them. The box should be lined with three or four thicknesses of newspaper, as paper is a nonconductor of heat and the eggs will not be affected by rapid changes in the temperature so readily. It is much better to place only one layer of eggs over the bottom of the tray, as they have to be turned each day. To turn the eggs, lay a row of them to one side and gently roll the rest over in their places and in this way the eggs will have been turned just half over, so that the part that was at the bottom the day before is now at the top. Paper makes a very good covering for the eggs, too. If they are left in the open air for ten days in a dwelling they will dry out more than they would were they left in the nest built upon the moist earth. The temperature at which they are kept should be near 60 degrees Fahrenheit. Eggs of ordinary fertility may be kept two weeks safely.

How to Fight Lice, Mites, Etc.

You will find that the poultryman who has much difficulty in raising his flock of young birds is generally so conceited about his own ability as a poultryman and his ability to analyze the causes of his trouble. No doubt this first statement is pretty harsh and will evoke criticism, but I mean just what I say, and the only qualification I wish to put on it is where a new beginner has let his enthusiasm lead him to undertake too much before he is thoroly familiar with the poultry business, and I am sure after you think back for several years of the failures and troubles among poultry raisers you will agree with me.

I am almost tempted to say that 90 per cent of the poultrymen would not know a head louse if they should see it. Again, 25 per cent do not know where to find the little red mites which make such ravages upon the fowls each year. I should say the same thing about the ordinary body louse, the least-harmful, altho the largest of all. Time and again I have been astonished upon visiting breeders of thorobred poultry—the fellows who claim to know all the "ins" and "outs" and tricks of the trade and all about the business, to hear them try to argue with me, when investigating the probable cause of the little chicks' weakness, that "that isn't a head louse, those are feathers." And then to look among the chicks' feathers for the little red mites, when, as a matter of fact, they have to be millions strong before they will be found during the day, and that is about the last place you will find them. Another fallacy is that the place to look for body lice is under the wing, when, again, as a matter of fact, the chick or adult fowl has to be literally alive with lice before you will find more than an occasional one under the wing.

Aside from faulty brooding, the two pests of the young chicks are lice and white diarrhea, and neither need cause the poultryman any concern whatever if he will first learn the seat of the trouble and then use preventitive methods instead of combative remedies after his flock is well in the grasp of one of these pests.

You might as well make up your mind that every species of louse and mite will appear some time or other during the season just as sure as you set a hen or operate an incuator, and don't be so conceited about your flock of thorobreds as to argue that as I hatch them in an incubator and raise them in a brooder away from all other poultry, therefore my chicks will not be infested with lice. Look out, you will be hit good and hard with ten thousand times ten thousand of those pesky mites before you know it. Like Topsy, they don't seem to have any starting point, but just grow.

White diarrhea will probably appear some time during the season, altho not such a certain and known quantity as lice. There are enough preventitive remedies on the market that are thoroly reliable, that every person attempting to raise little chicks should purchase a bottle or package before the chicks hatch and administer it as directed as soon as the chicks hatch and regularly every week or two until the chicks are good, big fellows, well feathered out, and then about once a month. Last year one of the severest cases of white diarrhea I ever saw and the only one of the season developed in a fully-feathered, healthy young cockerel nine weeks old and had it not been that I had a supply of the preventitive medicine on hand I would have certainly lost him before I could have ordered thru the mail and in turn received it.

For several seasons several years ago, I, too, went under the delusion that my chicks were being raised under perfect conditions, perfect feed, etc., and therefore I need not worry about lice or anything else and need not take any precaution about prevention, but experience is a good teacher and cures are hard to effect, so I retraced my steps, and I have been going on the assumption for several seasons now, like I did when I first commenced raising poultry that my chicks probably have few lice or white diarrhea, and I give them a dose "just to make sure, anyway," as my grandmother used to do to me when I would come in with wet feet, which would mean a bad cold if not taken in time.

Grease the little chicks' heads and throats with sweet oil when you take them off the nest or out of the machine. It is is easier to do then and does not take half the time, and it will last them for a couple of weeks, at least. Then, even if there are not signs of head lice at the end of that time, take an evening off and repeat the operation, and again in another two weeks. I found that a systematic treatment like this every two weeks is very much less nerve-racking than to worry for days after they commence to die, and fret and stew as to what to do, and whether you will ever raise one or not.

Scald out the brooder or brood coop every week or ten days with the hot soap-water left from the washing, and it will be better to add some strong lye. Get this water in every crack and crevice, underneath the floor as well as the walls and lid, and your worries about mites will be short-lived indeed. Scalding water kills the nits or eggs of these mites better than anything else, aside from fire, that I have ever tried. There are many good liquid disinfectants and louse-killers that may be added to water that are very fine also. Coal oil poured around in the cracks is also good. Remember the mites stay in the coop and only come out at night and suck the blood from the fowls. You will find them away down deep in the cracks or under the floor or at the ends of the roosts.

If a few body lice appear a little sweet oil under the vent of the little chicks, as well as about the throat and head, will soon put them out of commission.

Head lice are a species of tick. Body lice are scavengers and live on the offal of the skin. They cannot suck blood. The little red mites are mites, as the word implies, and live on the blood alone.

Prepare Early For Green Food and Shade.

During the early part of May plans should be made to provide the poultry yards with liberal supplies of green food and plenty of shade for the coming summer. If quantities of fresh lawn clippings can be had during hot months it probably will not be necessary to plan much further for the green food, but poultry enjoy so much to pick the greens fresh from the stem, and if only a small plot ten by ten feet can be fenced off in which to grow a little green food, it will serve to improve the general tone of the flock. It is the domestic fowl's habit to roam about in quest of food—not to tramp about on a bare plot of ground —during the whole season and, in keeping with nature's plans, the yard should be so arranged that half of it at least is under cultivation at one time growing a crop of some kind that fowls enjoy and into which they may be be released once a day at least for an hour or so. A plot of fresh earth under cultivation to which the fowls have access is a remedy for most ills of the poultry yard. If the poultry yard can not conveniently be divided into two parts for each pen of fowls and the flock turned into one or the other at will, then a corner or one end of the yard may be fenced off and spaded up for cultivation.

There are many different varieties of vegetation that poultry enjoy as green food. Indeed, the fowls are not at all particular, and, for this fact, it is all the easier for the poultry raiser to select some crop that is adapted to the location and soil as well as the season and length of time in which he has to grow it. Fowls are especially fond of short, tender blades of grass of almost any variety, of young oats and rye, of lettuce the many different kinds of clover, alfalfa, rape and even of young dandelion plants.

A crop of oats is desirable in the early spring and summer, when plenty of moisture is a certainty, but, when sown later in the summer, the crop is likely to be a failure unless it can be watered. Oats is the most satisfactory green food where the board inclosure, with wire netting top is used. Rye is sown only in the fall for early winter use.

All the surplus lettuce from the family garden and kitchen should be fed to the fowls, and when the patch in the garden becomes too tough for family use it should be fed to the flock as quickly as possible before it goes to seed and becomes useless.

Clover and alfalfa, like the grasses, require too long a time and too much work to be used by the small poultry raiser as an exclusive crop for the fowls, but where these succulent plants can be obtained and fed with little trouble they are most excellent green food.

Rape is one of the nutritious greens where moisture is a certainty, and it can be sown any time from April to August. It cannot be recommended too highly as green food, as it grows rapidly and will stand much more drought than anything else that can be planted. Rape is ready to use in three or four weeks, depending upon the time of year. The fowls may be allowed the run of the patch for a half hour or so every other day at first. After the growth is well established the time may be prolonged until the fowls can be kept in it all the time, and the other half of the yard spaded up and sown in the same manner. The winter or biennial varieties should be sown. The dwarf Essex or English is the most widely cultivated.

A very good plan in sowing a plot for green food for poultry is to mix several different kinds of seeds. In this way the fowls get what they crave most and the conditions under which they live are made much more natural. A mixture of oats, lettuce, millet and rape furnishes an excellent food and a quick growing crop. A few cowpea seeds may be added, as the fowls like the leaves from this plant.

Feed a variety of foods, not because "Variety is the spice of life," but because the hens will then be sure to get some of the things they need.

There is little excuse for the bare sun beaten poultry yard so often seen when natural shade can be so easily provided with a little forethought in the spring. The poultry yard can be made as attractive as the front lawn with a few landscape gardening rules applied. The soil about the yard is generally very rich and very little care need be given the shade producing plants protected from the fowls. Of course, the orchard is the ideal place for fowls, but. lacking this, shade from shrubs, small fruit trees, vines and different tall annual plants will serve. Quince and lilac bushes may be grown in the poultry yard if they are inclosed with a small fence the first two years. A row of blackberry and raspberry bushes may be planted along the south fence. Morning glory and wild cucumber vines will make profuse shade on the wire netting fence in a few weeks. The tall varieties of sunflowers hide unattractive places and the seed is the best poultry conditioner and fattener that can be had. When used in combination with vines, the sunflower makes a very pleasing background.

Mineral Matter in the Food is Absolutely Necessary.

When the breeding stock is deprived of the proper amount of mineral food the egg content will soon be imperfect and the supply diminish. As a result chicks die in the shell or the eggs produce weak chicks. There may be a good egg yield and still an imperfect egg content from lack of mineral matter other than lime. Lack of suitable mineral food may also be a factor in causing poor fertility or even sterility.

Fowls will live and apparently thrive on soils where there is practically no natural grit, but under such conditions where grit is not supplied they will eat large quantities of the soft earth. Young stock raised on such soil may be coop fed or crate fed for from two to three weeks and keep in good condition with no grit or earth supplied and no other mineral food except that contained in the grain and green stuff fed. Continue the experiment one to three weeks longer, feeding, as far as possible, food containing little or no mineral food and the confined birds will get out of condition and die. A fowl positively deprived of all mineral food will usually die in from one month to six weeks. Mineral food supplied in fine powder form will permit continuing the experiment for an indefinite period, but hard, sharp grit has not been found necessary to life.

Between 5 and 6 per cent of the fowl's body, including feathers, is mineral matter and should the carcass of a six-pound fowl be burned and all the ash saved it will weigh approximately five to five and one-half ounces.

Eggs contain between 11 and 12 per cent mineral matter. Of this amount about 11 per cent is the shell and about 1 per cent is contained in the egg contents and contains all the mineral elements needed to perfect a living, hatchable chick. The shell of the egg is mostly calcium carbonate (lime).

The average shell will weigh about two ounces. A good six-pound hen ought to yield at least twelve dozen eggs in twelve months—eighteen pounds of egg in one year. The twelve dozen eggs would contain about two pounds of mineral matter.

The more important minerals found in the fowl's body and in eggs are: Calcium, sodium, potassium, magnesium, phosphorus, sulphur, silicon and iron. They are not found in a free state, but in chemical combinations as carbonates, phosphates, sulphates, chlorides, etc. Salt (sodium chloride) is an important consistent of the blood. Potassium chloride is found in the red blood cells and in the muscles. Potasium phosphate in the brain and nerve tissue. Calcium, magnesium and silicon in cartilages, bones and feathers; iron in the blood.

Mineral food not only supplies the fowl's body with mineral nourishment necessary to maintenance, repair and upbuilding of the various parts, but it also assists very materially in the active process of nutrition by promoting cell metabolism—the actual act or process by which living cells take up and properly use food material brought to them and reject or throw off the waste material and is aided by the presence of essential mineral foods.

It is difficult to make an accurate estimate of the amount of mineral food needed daily by a normal fowl. Not less than two pounds is needed for eggs alone in a year. A large amount of that which is eaten is not usable and must be passed out. The droppings of a healthy hen for a year will yield from eight to ten pounds of mineral matter. The fowl's digestive organs select what can be used and is required and reject the balance.

The average minimum daily intake of mineral food for an adult fowl is about half an ounce, or in one year, approximately not less than eleven or twelve pounds.

.A failure to supply plenty of oyster shells and cracked bone to laying hens will result in soft shelled eggs and a tendency to egg cating. When a fowl eagerly eats stones, glass and other gritty substances it is striving to satisfy a craving for some needed mineral food with which it is not supplied. A very small amount of the hard grits is assimilated by the digestive organs of the fowl and serve for little purpose. The fowls should be supplied with plenty of cracked oyster shells, fine gravel or coarse sand, ground bone and mica crystal grit.

Growing chicks need plenty of mineral food to supply the needs of their rapidly growing bodies. They particularly need shells and raw dry bone to supply material for bone making and other tissues. They need sand to supply silicon for the feathers. If the chick is deprived of these, weak legs, slow feathering, crooked breast bones and other deformities is the result.

Cutting the Cost of Feed Stuffs.

Few poultrymen keep an account of just how much their feed costs them in a year. Did you ever stop to get even a rough estimate of just what your feed bills will amount to in a year's time? If you have not, it will pay you. It is hardly worth while for me to argue with you about the value of buying feeds in large quantities but it may be worth while to dwell upon the advisability of buying feeds at the proper time.

There is hardly a place in the United States where corn and wheat are not practical feeds for fowls and when I use the term practical I mean economical in the broadest sense. The American farmer feeds little else beside corn the greater part of the year and if he raises wheat he may manage to save the screenings from the threshing for the fowls. This is not practical because, altho corn, for example, is one of the best proportioned grains yet it is not well balanced enough to feed it and nothing else and expect profit from the investment.

The poultryman on the other hand knows that it pays to feed a variety and as nearly a balanced ration as possible. Too many poultrymen, however, feed expensive feeds when it is not necessary. "It is not what a man makes but what he saves" is a favorite axiom. So with good judgment used in the mere matter of feeding and buying feeds quite a saving can be made during the year.

August is the great wheat threshing month. Threshing begins many places early in July but by August wheat is on the market. I do not know how many poultrymen watch the market page of the daily papers but it will pay you if you feed any considerable number of fowls. I have found it a pretty safe rule to follow to lay in a supply of wheat during August. Year in and year out you will find it about as cheap then as any time during the whole year.

The poultryman should have large bins provided and keep an eye open for bargains in poultry wheat. You do not need to buy first class wheat but often can get bargains in wheat that may have wild onions in it or some other slight defect that makes it hard to dispose of. Wheat of this kind can generally be gotten at a very low figure, considering the real market price of first class wheat at the time, and if the poultryman is wise enough to have bin capacity he can cut a big hole in his feed bill of the year by buying a large quantity of such wheat.

Sometimes it can be bought of the farmer and again a miller or grain dealer gets such a quantity of just such wheat on his hands that he is only too glad to make a price on it for quick sale. Every poultryman knows how to make a good scratch grain and there is nothing better for the body of the scratch grain than wheat. Occasionally, those living in close proximity to extensive farming districts and who can get in touch with the farmers at threshing time can get large quantities of wheat screenings for almost nothing.

Later in the fall a supply of whole corn can be laid in at a profit. Remember ground grains are liable to heat and especially ground corn. But it is always safe to lay in a good supply of whole corn and nothing makes a better last feed of the day during the cold winter months than whole corn. Several bushels can be fed this way and if the corn is bought right quite a saving can be made.

It is hardly ever profitable or wise to buy oats in any quantity because it is not a very good feed by itself, altho there is no better growing feed than oats. The hull on the oats is the great drawback to more extensive feeding by poltrymen. Pin head or hulled oats make a splendid feed.

Then again the wholesale grocer may have a bargain in scratch grains of some well known brand which he is closing out and has a few sacks left. Wholesale feed men in all the large cities send out prices of feed stuffs each month and it is well to have your name on their list. You will find many dollars can be saved, even with a flock of 50 fowls during the year, if feeds are bought for cash at the right time in quantities.

For Winter Results and Poultry Success.

The problem of where to start to make a success of the poultry business is as much a question as the old one, "Which Was First, The Hen or The Egg." So in advising beginners or trying to help these with many years' experience out of difficult problems always reverts into the advice so often quoted, "Get Good Strong Healthy Stock or Strong Germed Eggs Full of Vitality," yet this advice seems preplexing, for when are we sure we have the stock described as filling the bill and if we have the stock described how are we sure they will lay the kind of coveted eggs desired? Between the hen and the chick there is always plenty of room for failure and also between the chick and the adult there is plenty of room for failure or if not utter failure weakening the vitality.

So, in attempting to give the reader an idea of the condition his young stock should be in to make a success of the winter work, I am compelled to go back to the parent stock of the chicks you are working with and even back two or three generations and state that the chicks should be hatched from eggs laid by good healthy vigorous stock and the eggs from this flock should be picked and cared for with care and the chicks should never have a "set back" of a single day during their summer existence. What I mean by a "set back" is that they should not be annoyed a single day with lice, with the bacteria or white diarrhea. No matter if they only have a slight attack it will always weaken them to a certain extent, with confinement in small bare runs with no shade, with crowding, with a lack of proper brooding when young, and so on through the whole catagory of evils that are the hard luck agents of so many poultrmen.

I may be a crank on the subject of raising chicks under ideal natural surroundings, but I have good reasons to believe and believe the experience of poultrymen much older than I as well as science will bear me out in the statement that even keeping small chicks confined after sunup causing them to fret and worry will take several hours a day growth from them. The change in the quality of milk given by cows when annoyed or worried is a fair example of what I am trying to impress upon the grower of young fowls. Therefore, it is my aim to so raise my fowls that they never give a cheep of the note of dissatisfaction, annoyance or unnatural hunger. With life sailing on for them under this even tenor from the day they are hatched until they are five months of age when most of the pullets are laying, I believe I am justified in claiming with due conversation that I have gained a month in size and 50 per cent or more in vigor and stamina over the chicks that have had a slight attack of white diarrhea, six to three dozen head lice for a week or two before the owner noticed them waning in spirits, two to three months' annoyance of mites at night and long confinement in foul coops after sunup, as well as confinement in small bare runs during the day, no matter how well fed. These are the little things that go to make the winter's work successful and profitable or unsuccessful and unprofitable as the individual case may be.

Many poultry men gage their success for the season by the number of chicks they had to die, but taking the sensible view of it when a chick is so sick it dies with a reasonable degree of surety should we not find several more in the same flock that are so sick they have lost several week's growth. We should, therefore, not watch out for the deaths in our flocks before we become alarmed, but rather live with them so that we will notice the change in their spirits when a chick suffers its first annoyance no matter from what source.

With such a flock you can go into the winter with great assurance if the same care and attention to details is followed as in babyhood. The cockerels should have been removed at the first sign of annoyance. The pullets should never be frightened or chased any more than a modern dairyman would permit such a thing with his cows. Young fowls should be taught to follow like sheep with the use of a little grain and I find it much easier to take them where I want them by this method rather than bunching them up and frightening a week's growth out of them. For this reason I like to move the brood coops they are in gradually up to the winter house so that late in the fall or whenever, according to their age largely, I want to change them from their colony coop to the house for the winter they are so accustomed to roosting near the house that the first night I remove the colony coop away entirely they hardly know the change and go right in the house. The change has been so gradual that they never are annoyed and worried a single hour. These attentions to trifles and details might be called nonsense and theory by some, but by actual experience the more I live with fowls the more I find this attention to small details pays. It brings the pullets up to their very best and yet does not bring on egg production too soon when they are far undeveloped nor does it pay less well with the cockerels whether for broilers or breeders. Kindness and attention to details with any kind of domestic fowls or animals will pay handsomely coupled with experience. We cannot really be kind to our wards until we have experience and know how. The bee keeper even preaches kindness and attention to details and it is common knowledge that the bees disturbed and annoyed for a few minutes will lose the better part of a day's work.

The pullets then, when in the laying house, should be taught to use the house as soon as cold weather begins. Do not wait until the ground is frozen before the house is gone over for the winter, and plenty of litter added to the house. To carry the pullets from the late fall into the winter, laying all the time, is a trick, so to speak, and the trick is none other than watching carefully the wants of the young fowls and supplying every need as winter closes in about them. Early in the fall on cold mornings or rainy weather, accustom the pullets to use the litter by giving their scratch grain in it. The dry mash hoppers of course, are in the winter house and kept full of mash all the time. This makes the poultry house the most thriving place the young fowls can find and they will take to it like ducks to water. When real cold weather sets in the fowls hardly notice the doors are closed and they are confined all day. Thus, their nervous sytsem does not have a single shock, they never fret and worry at being confined causing the egg yield to stop right at the time cold weather commences and eggs are high, but they go right on laying and will lay through the winter if the house is built substantially and well ventilated and lighted and the proper care and feed is given the young pullets. Compare this method with that in vogue with many where the young stock is all over the place roosting in the barn and on fences and shifting for themselves and left thus until the snow overtakes them and they have to be lifted from their roosts and taken to a laying house. Of course they will worry at being confined and it will take two months to get them accustomed and to laying again right while eggs are highest. Do not understand me to be against fowls shifting for themselves as much as possible. This is all right, but at the same time while they are out leading a natural life in the open I want to keep them so under my control and feed them so regularly at their proper place that I can handle them at any time and they will roost at night where I invite them. Sounds a little unreasonable, but it can be done and done easily by observing the fowl's instinct, following the laws of nature and attention to the little things that make life worth living, even for the lowly fowl.

As a final warning, do not crowd the young fowls and when they want to roost give them a flat board to roost on.

How to Get Plenty of Eggs in Winter.

The natural time of the year for the hen to lay is in the spring and summer, but any variety or breed of fowls so popular today can be made to produce eggs during the dead of winter with proper care and feeding. Certain natural desirable characteristics have been fostered and intensified tho by selection and mating until there are now breeds that excel in some particulars over others.

When the demand for eggs exceeds the supply the price of eggs advances as a natural consequence. The egg farmer has solved the problem and has made the getting of eggs a scientific certainty when the prices are high, much to his profit. The family keeping just a few hens may do the same thing and make the average egg yield per hen even greater, because fowls do better in smaller numbers and better attention can be afforded the small flock.

The egg farmer places his fowls under conditions as nearly like spring as possible with the exception of the temperature, as it has been found that hens do not require warm quarters. They thrive in dry, windproof quarters without drafts and with as much sunshine and fresh air as possible. He feeds them a well balanced ration, which is as near like the hens would get were they roaming about over broad fields in the summer time. The bugs and worms the fowls get during the summer play quite an important part in influencing the egg yield.

To take the place of the bugs and worms some form of meat must be fed. Some one of the by-products of beef is the cheapest and most satisfactory. In isolated country districts milk can be fed to advantage, but milk is almost as hard to obtain and as high priced as eggs for the average city or town dweller. The packing houses are near tho, and beef scraps or dried beef blood prepared especially for chickens can be obtained at any of the seed or feed stores at very reasonable rates when purchased in 100 pound bags and fed as easily as grain.

Beef scraps are superior to dried blood. If of good quality it will keep indefinitely if kept dry. Its appearance is hardly what the name might suggest, as the scraps after being cooked thoroly tender are ground into coarse bits so it can be fed in the mash. Mix the mash in the following proportions by emptying the meal on a clean floor or have the feed man do it before delivery and shoveling it about, dry, until thoroly mixed. Keep the feed in barrels away from rats and feed as needed by scalding a sufficient quantity for the flock. A good mixture is as follows: Chop feed, 40 lbs.; middlings, 22 lbs.; beef scraps, 15 lbs.

Chop feed is composed of half and half oats and corn ground together. Middlings is a by-product of wheat flour—the heart or middle of the wheat and the richest part, but which modern milling methods has decreed shall not go into the flour, sacrificing nutritive properties for whiteness. Bran is the hull or outer covering of wheat.

Chickens must have some kind of green food along with their grain during the winter if many eggs are expected. Beef scraps, green cut bone, blood meal or chopped raw beef will take the place of the bugs and worms they pick up during the summer, but something must also be provided to take the place of the tender blades of grass picked here and there. Grains are too concentrated in themselves to form the whole diet for fowls. With a crop filled with nothing but grains the starch in them becomes pasty and sticky after becoming moist and will not move along easily thru the fowl's peculiarly formed alimentary canal unless there is some bulky substance mixed with the food. In fact, it requires very much less food if bulky green foods of some kind are fed regularly, and, of course, they are much cheaper.

At first thot it would seem almost impossible to have a supply of green food during the winter in our northern and central states without considerable cost. There are several different ways of supplying this part of the ration, tho. Apple parings and cabbage leaves which would otherwise be wasted in the kitchen can be chopped up with a vegetable cutter in pieces small enough for the fowls to swallow, and they form an excellent substitute for the grasses of summer. Heads of cabbage may be hung up in the scratching shed so the fowls will be required to jump for them. This also provides exercise. Care should be taken, tho, not to feed too much cabbage, as it will give the eggs a peculiar flavor. If turnips are plentiful they also may be fed in this manner. In the last few years alfalfa has been placed upon the market in the form of a dry bulky meal for poultry. A quantity of the meal is scalded with hot water the night before it is intended for use. It turns as green as grass as soon as it is scalded, but it should be left covered tightly for several hours. It should then be mixed with mash food to form about one-fourth of the quantity of the bulk.

Pure, clean clover hay is equally good chopped up and scalded and fed in this manner or a bale of clover hay may be left in some out of the way place for the fowls when it will soon be found the leaves will all be picked from the stems. Then the bale may be torn apart. It will surprise some to think of fowls eating hay, but they will actually eat all the leaves of the clover stems, so much do they relish bulky food. The cow beet or mangel wurzel form a very cheap and efficient green food for poultry, but they can scarcely ever be purchased on the market. If you want a supply of green food for your fowls for next year sow a small quantity of the seed along in July or engage some farmer to grow some for you. If you live in the suburbs possibly there is a hothouse near which grows lettuce during the winter. The waste leaves may be obtained at small cost. Sprouted oats or wheat makes another good form of green food for winter use. The grain is soaked in lukewarm water over night and then placed in a shallow box or pan in a two-inch layer and the box kept in a moderately warm temperature for ten days or two weeks or until the young plants reach a height of two or three inches.

The Louse Question a Live Issue in the Dead of Winter.

Those who should really read this article, no doubt will feel on reading the headlines that it is another of those theories of inexperienced poultry writers and leave it at that.

All the articles on the lice problem that I have found raise a loud warning about the pest during the spring and summer and fall and seem to take it for granted that with cold weather lice will be a minus factor. But such is not the case. I had poultry for several years before I became alive to the importance of the lice problem in the dead of the winter and its relation to the general health and efficiency of the flock. It is then the large body lice get in their deadly work. The awkward and ungainly young cockerels and old cocks are the first to fall an easy prey to these big body lice. Old hens and the light laying class of young pullets are last to contract body lice because of their neat and thrifty habits about their personal cleanliness.

The poulterer must have as keen and educated an eye and as quick to note symptoms and what they indicate as the skilled physician.

Did you ever see head lice? This is an insult to the average poultryman for he knows head lice from feathers. Many farmers and back-lotters do not know a head louse when they see it. You have probably seen this class of people. Let me ask another question. Did you ever see a young cockerel or cock that had all the fine particles of feathers of his entire body eaten off by body lice? If you have not, you have not been a very careful observer. To the experienced eye it does not take very strong light to know when you have such a bird in hand.

It is generally known that body lice do not penetrate the skin or suck the blood, that head lice are a species of tick and live as such with their heads burrowed in the flesh, that the little red mites also are equipped with skin penetrating mouths and live upon blood. But what do the body lice live upon you ask? They are scavengers, if you please, and live on the offals of the fowl. They depend upon moisture from the eyes and vent and for food upon the growing feathers and the constantly shedding epidermis or skin.

Fowls bury their heads under the wings when they sleep or rather just above it in the feathers. In the early fall and winter fowls and especially young fowls are susceptible to colds. Their nostrils run just as in humans. During the night this excreta is deposited on the feathers on either side just above the wing secondaries. This makes a sticky, filthy mass of feathers in a short time and for the time being a veritable paradise for those big body lice. If you have never seen these symptoms in your flock be a little more careful in your examination of your backward cockerels.

I have made it a practice for several years to paint a circle of blue ointment, using a portion about the size of a pea on each fowl twice a year. This is about all that is necessary for the body lice as a general rule. The fowls will soon be entirely free of this pest if this treatment is followed for the fowls will keep lice from getting moisture from the eye by industriously scratching when one runs up his neck. The louse dies of thirst as a result. provided your fowls do not have a slight cold and the lice get their supply of moisture from the feathers above and back of the wings.

Colds are responsible for the lice and the lice are responsible for colds. This is why youngsters contracting colds in the fall do not seem to yield to the best of treatment. It is because in a short time after getting a cold they become alive with lice, and lice so weaken their systems that no amount of cold and roup treatment will cure them. You are lucky if you do not have a few of this class in your flock from which you can gather practical information at once upon the winter louse question. On these fowls you will find the feather in a different condition than on a healthy fowl and it is because the feathers have been constantly preyed upon since early in the fall by lice and the tender particles of feather eaten as they protrude from the skin just as your hens eat the tender blades of grass in the spring as they first come thru the ground. The skin will be rough and scaly, too, on a fowl in this condition. Yet I find many cannot detect these symptoms in their fowls as a result birds are said to go light, have rheumatism, cholera and numerous other diseases.

This fall I went to inspect a flock of a friend and customer while on a trip, and this friend complained of a cock two years old that I had sold him as a cockerel. Stated he was sick and stiff as if he had rheumatism. Did not know what was the matter with him. This party, naturally a very careful and clean man about his premises had utterly failed to note the lice on his cock. He was deeply chagrined over the affair and wrote me in a couple of weeks the bird was nearly back in normal condition. I was in a show a few days ago and in looking over a nice string of birds of a certain experienced breeder, heard him remark that a certain cock, pointing him out, was not making the show bird he expected and seemed to be off condition continually. I examined the bird and found him a mass of lice and his feathers eaten as above described until there was no nice downy fluff beneath any more at all in any portion of his body.

A fitting climax to the louse question in winter came a few days ago when a $25.00 Rhode Island cock was returned to a friend from a customer in the west. The cock had been shipped early in September in fine condition and well worth the money. The customer was more than pleased as evidenced by letters which my friend proudly displayed. Later the customer wrote that the cock was off his feet and seemed to be stiff and unable to stand and in bad condition. My friend asked me what to suggest. I stated I was afraid it was rheumatism caused by overfeeding of a high priced bird and subsequent liver trouble which brought on the rheumatism. I suggested Dr. King's New Life Pills which I have found better for slight attacks of this kind than anything else. Nothing seemed to help the bird so the customer wrote and he finally became so disgusted that he wrote my friend that he could have the bird back by paying the express and added, "Keep the $25.00. I am stung." I was so familiar with the whole transaction and the bird in particular that I urged my friend to take the customer up on his proposition to ferret out what was wrong if the bird came back or to shut up the customer if he was attempting to defraud the seller by his constant kicking.

The bird came back. He could not stand up in the coop. Not in a long time have I seen such a sight. My friend at first was so dumbfounded at the haggard condition of the fowl that he did not attempt to analyze the difficulty. He called my attention to the bird being back, and in line with my recent experiences with others with lousy fowls, I suggested that he look for body lice. The next day I heard from him and he declared he could not have stretched his imagination enough to believe so many lice could be on one fowl. Louse powder removed the lice, and Licene was applied about the vent. The cock ate all the corn from two fair sized ears of corn the next day. I warned my friend not to overfeed the glutten. He is on his feet and will make a winner yet at the late shows. Think of a poultryman with a big letter head buying a $25.00 bird and letting him slip thru his hands in three short months like that for the lack of ordinary attention.

Use plenty of powder on backward birds that muss up their feathers about their wings with the excreta from their nostrils and use Licene on all your birds twice or three times a year as directed. I use Averneous Carbolineum on the roosts once a year or once in two years for mites. Put it on hot. One application will keep mites out of your houses three years but it is well to use it once a year. The old fashioned way of spraying with dips and disinfecting with sulphur fumes and what not is a waste of time. Licene and Averneous Carbolineum, advertised in all journals are all anyone needs and you only have to use the one twice a year and the other once in two years to be absolutely free of lice and mites the year round.

Building Exhibition and Shipping Coops.

When I planned to make my first exhibit at a poultry show I was quite at a loss to know what kind of a coop I would need to show my birds in, how big they should be, what they should be made of, etc. It took quite a lot of searching before I could even find the dimensions of a standard coop. Today there are any number of firms who sell exhibition coops knocked down, but all finished except putting the nails and screws in them. A great many poultry fanciers like to build their own poultry houses and coops for hens and chicks, and likewise would have the spare time and much enjoy building their own exhibition coops.

It does not take many tools to make an exhibition coop,

but to make nice, neat looking coops that will show off the fine birds they are to contain well, pains must be taken in their construction and time taken for accuracy in dimensions.

The first thing to find out after you have decided to show at a certain show is whether they furnish exhibition coops or require the exhibitor to furnish them. If the exhibitor is required to furnish them figure out how many single specimens you intend to show as well as pens. From the ink sketch of coop and the sketch showing frame and floor construction the mode of constructing an exhibition coop can be easily seen. The wooden rods from which to make the front of the coop are ordered at a nearby planing mill, and should be a little less than a half inch thick. Or if preferred iron wire may be used and painted as the wooden rods are.

The dimensions for a standard exhibition coop which will accommodate either single birds or pairs, is 24x24x30 inches high and the pen size is the same in height and width, but 40 inches long.

You will note the little drop door at the bottom of the coop. The floor may be made to slide in as a drawer in this door to facilitate rapid cleaning, or the floor may be built to the coop and cleaned thru this little door with a miniature hoe being made by tacking a piece of galvanized iron to a broom handle. I have built several coops together making a string as long as ten feet, but I find five or six foot sections more satisfactory. The beauty in making coops of several in a section is that they can be made stronger, and they are not tossed about with as much ease by the strong arm expressman as the single pen size coops. The coops are thus insured better treatment while in transit as well as the birds.

When shipping a string of birds in exhibition coops it is advisable to tack lath quite freely over the canvas part to make it as unhandy as possible for the drayman to shove a foot thru the side of the coop and release a fine bird or two.

The top of the coop may be covered either with canvas or slats, but I prefer the slats as they admit more light and make the coop more substantial. The front of the coop should be covered with drop curtain of muslin securely fastened while the birds are in transit. Inquisitive loafers at the depots cannot torment the birds, and if the weather is at all chilly or cold, as it generally is during the show season, the birds should be thus protected to keep them from being exposed to drafts and taking cold and roup.

In building exhibition coops the thot should be constantly in mind to make them as light as possible, and yet have them strong and durable. Light, soft pine is the best for frame work

 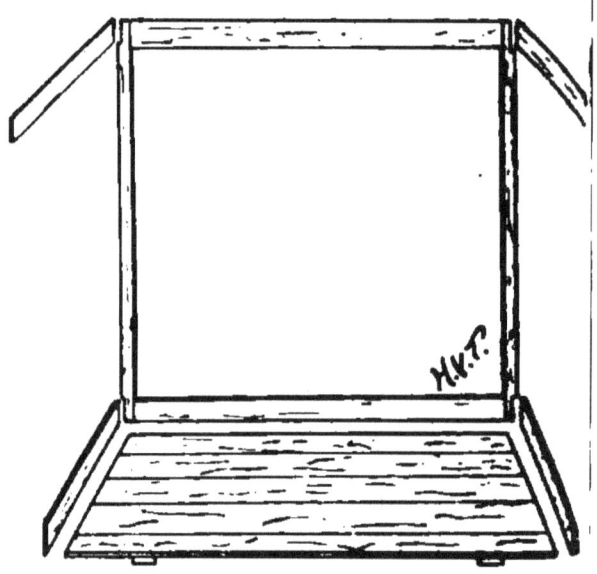

and hard pine for the rods. If the coop seems weak after it is put together it may be strengthened by twisting wires across as is done in strengthening old chairs.

When shipping securely fasten the drinking and other cups on the inside of the coops and tie down the doors. Never use anything but nice, clean rye or wheat straw; oats will do, in bedding down the coops. I never will forget my first experience in this line. I had not been to a single good poultry show before my first attempt at exhibiting. I built my own coops, and they were the best in the show, as I learned when I got to attend the last day, and I had conditioned my own birds according to information received in the poultry journals, and my birds proved to be in better condition than any in the class, but the boys had one laugh on me in that I put shavings and sawdust in my coop for bedding instead of straw. The birds got a lot of the sawdust in their plumage in shipping, but that did not keep me from winning four out of a possible five firsts. The sawdust gave me away, tho, as an amateur exhibitor.

Where coops are furnished for show by the association the birds should be shipped in shipping coops built like the illustration. They, too, should be made as light as possible in order to keep down express charges. I like to use as many lath in their construction as possible, and use good, stiff cardboard or corrugated paper from post toasties or other cereal shipping boxes to line the inside with. The cardboad is light and much better than gunny sacking or canvas. A shipping coop should be provided every single bird for it is very unsafe to ship two or three together on account of possible crowding and suffocation. If you ship a pen in exhibition coop the cock and a hen or two should be shipped separately in shipping coops.

The shipping coops, as well as exhibition coops, should be painted with some odd paint with a distinguishing mark on every side. You won't have to look for shipping tags on every coop in a dark hall piled high with coops on the last evening of the show then to find your shipping coops. You can tell yours by the yellow or white initials at a glance ten feet away. The address in full should also be painted in small letters on the coop so if the tags are lost they will not go astray. I learned this valuable lesson one time at a Chicago show when I found the assistants had traded similar coops and likewise a cockerel with me to a party in another state. It took another week to get my bird and he his.

Home Preservation of Eggs.

The high prices of fresh eggs in the late fall and winter make it desirable to have some simple, clean, cheap and reliable method of preserving the low priced spring and summer eggs for home consumption during the winter. Such a process would allow the poultryman farmer to preserve cheap eggs for his own consumption while he could sell his fresh eggs in the winter time at high prices. It would allow the consumer to buy eggs when low in price and save buying many when the prices are high. On a commercial scale this is done by means of cold storage, but this method is not practicable in the home. The price of cold storage eggs furthermore is determined by the price of fresh eggs and is, as a rule, much higher than the cost of storage.

The spoiling of eggs is due to the entrance of air, carrying germs of decomposition through the shell. Normally the shell has a surface coating of mucilaginous matter, which prevents the entrance of these harmful organisms into the egg for a considerable time. But if this coating is removed or softened by washing or otherwise the keeping quality of the egg is much reduced. These facts explain why the common methods of preservation have not been entirely successful, and suggest that the methods employed should be based upon the idea of protecting and rendering more effective the natural coating of the shell, so that air bearing germs of decomposition may be completely excluded.

The age of eggs may be approximately judged by taking advantage of the fact as they grow older their density decreases through evaporation of moisture. A new laid egg placed in a vessel of brine made of the proportion of one ounce of salt to one pint of water will at once sink to the bottom. An egg one day old will sink below the surface, but not to the bottom, while one three days old will swim just immersed in the liquid. If more than three days old, the egg will float on the surface, the amount of shell exposed increasing with age; and if two weeks old, only a little of the shell will dip in the liquid.

Many methods of preservation have been tried by many people and various experiment stations. Some of these have been packing the eggs in salt, oats, bran, peat dust, or wood ashes; covering them with parafine, vaseline, butter, lard or a solution of Salicylic acid and glycerine; varnishing with collodion or shellac; storing on shelves and in racks in cool places; wrapping in paper; sterilized by being immersed in boiling water a few seconds; treated with a solution of permanganate of potash or alum and packing in salt brine, lime water and water glass solutions.

Recently in Germany, twenty methods of preserving eggs were tested. Three methods which were found to be reliable were varnishing with vaseline, placing the eggs in lime water or water glass solutions. Of the three methods, preservation in a solution of water glass is especially recommended by the North Dakota experiment station, since varnishing the eggs with vaseline is time consuming and treatment with lime water sometimes communicates to the egg a disagreeable odor and taste. In most packed eggs, after a little time, the yolk settles to one side. and the egg is then inferior in quality. In eggs preserved four or five months in water glass the yolk retained its normal position in the egg, and in taste they were not distinguished from fresh, unpacked store eggs.

Water glass (soluble silicate of sodium) is a pale yellow, odorless, syrupy liquid. It may be obtained from most druggists at from 60 cents to 90 cents a gallon. Use only boiled water, to which after cooled, add 1 pint of water glass to fifteen parts of water. This should be sufficient to cover about fifteen dozen eggs in a four gallon crock.

The lime water mixture. Shake three pounds of good quick lime in a small amount of water, then add the milklime thus formed to three gallons of water. Keep the mixture well stirred for a day, then allow the excess lime to settle and use only the clear fluid.

Only absolutely fresh, clear, unwashed, sound eggs with smooth, firm shells are suitable for preserving by these methods. Infertile eggs are preferred as they keep better than fertile eggs. Any dirty, stale, cracked, or thin shelled eggs should be discarded as they are liable to spoil and affect the good eggs around them. Any eggs that float in the liquid should be removed as floating indicates that the contents of the egg are shrunken, leaving a large air cell. Such eggs are usually stale, cracked or thin shelled.

Any earthenware, glass or wooden jar, tub or barrel may be used as a container, depending upon the number of eggs to be preserved, metal containers must not be used as the solution will attack and corrode them. Wooden kegs or barrels should not have nails protruding through as even this small amount of metal will spoil the surrounding eggs. All vessels used must be absolutely clean and sweet because eggs are very susceptible to odors and taints of any nature. Scald the vessels with boiling water just before using, taking special care with those made of wood.

The eggs may be placed carefully in the vessels small ends down and the solution of water glass or lime water poured over them, or the vessel may be filled about one-half full with the liquid and the eggs carefully placed in as gathered. The latter method is preferable as it allows of packing the eggs just as soon as they are laid; also any eggs that would naturally float may be removed as they will not be held down by the heavy eggs above them. The liquid rises as the eggs are put in, but at least two inches of the preservative should be above the eggs at all times. In the lime water method a very little of the sediment should be added to insure a constantly saturated solution. A thin, white crust appearing on a lime water solution is due to the formation of calcium carbonate coming in contact with the air. This will do no harm if there is lime sediment present and should be left untouched as it will prevent further crust formation. Vessels containing eggs in preservatives should be kept in a cool, well ventilated place such as a good cellar and be covered to prevent evaporation of the preservative. A new mixture should be prepared for each lot of eggs.

One gallon of water glass as purchased will make enough preservative to preserve from 75 to 100 dozen eggs. The cost of preservation by the water glass method is less than 1 cent a dozen eggs, not taking into consideration the cost of the container, and by the lime water method still cheaper. The water glass mixture should be used, however, whenever the water glass may be secured at less than $1 a gallon.

Eggs preserved by either of these methods may be used to replace strictly fresh eggs, for nearly all cooking purposes.

In boiling it may be necessary to pierce the shell at the large end to prevent cracking of the shell as preservative seals the pores of the shell and prevents the escape of the gases, which is possible in the strictly fresh egg. In frying and poaching, some trouble may be found because of the yolk breaking. In some instances the whites may not whip up as firmly as fresh eggs, but this quality as well as the firmness of the yolk depends largely upon the condition of the egg when packed. Eggs which have firm yolks and whites when packed usually give no trouble when cooked. For those purposes where no objection is raised to a broken yolk, as in cakes, custards, and omelettes, the preserved egg is fully the equal of the strictly fresh egg and may be used at a great saving in cost.

If a white deposit is found upon the eggs when removed from either the water glass or lime water solutions, it may be readily removed by holding the egg under a faucet or pouring water over them.

Linebreeding.

Several years ago the veteran poultry breeder of the United States, I. K. Felch of Massachusetts, worked out a system of breeding by which a pair of fowls are taken that are as near ideal as we can find and by breeding as indicated by the chart shown herewith, three distinct strains are established. These strains are so remotely related that for all practical purposes they may be called unrelated.

So many get linebreeding confused with inbreeding that it might be well to distinguish between the two. Linebreeding is the systematic and careful breeding and mating of the offspring of an ideal pair of fowls after a manner indicated by the chart. Inbreeding is the breeding of the brothers and sisters one or more generations, promiscuously, or of sire on daughter and granddaughter, and

Drawn By H.V.Tormohlen   After I K.Felch

then possibly the crossing of the brother on sister again from this mating. Inbreeding might be anything where the same blood is intermingled generation after generation without going about it in the systematic way used in line breeding.

In the chart lot 1 represents the original male and lot 2 the original female. Then by crossing 1 and 2 the result is group 3, which possesses equal parts of the blood of the original pair. Selecting the best pullet from 3 and mating to her sire 1, group 4 is produced, which contains three-fourths of the blood of the original sire and one-fourth of the blood of the original dam. In a like manner the best cockerel from 3 mated to his dam (2) produces group 5, which is made up of three-fourths of the blood of the original dam and one-fourth of the original sire.

Proceeding in a similar manner by mating the original parents to their offspring in the third generation we obtain group 6 and 7 offspring which contains either seven-eights of the blood of the original sire and one-eighth the blood of the original dam; or seven-eighths blood of the original dam and one-eighth the blood of the sire, as the case may be.

Thus the blood of the original sire has been practically eliminated from the female line, and the blood of the original dam from the male line. If the original parents were still in breeding condition the blood of each could be intensified to fifteen-sixteenths in fifth generation. To obtain the original cross, however, it is only necessary to select parents from the corresponding groups on each side of the line. For instance, a cockerel from group 6 mated to pullets from group 7 will produce in the fifth generation group 9, which contains mathematically one-half the blood of the original pair. Similar results can be obtained by selecting parents from 4 and 5.

The fifth and sixth generations, as shown in the chart, indicate only a few of the possible groups that may be obtained from various matings.. Thus if the original sire and dam cannot be used for breeding purposes beyond the fourth generation, their blood may be maintained in fifteen-sixteenths of its intensity by choosing parents from groups 4 and 6, or 5 and 7, to produce groups 8 and 10 respectfully. Then parents chosen from groups 8 and 10 will produce group 13, which is again mathematically one-half the blood of the original pair, and the original offspring again reproduces as far as the blood lines are concerned.

By choosing parents from groups 7 and 10, twenty-seven thirty-seconds of the blood of the original dam, and five thirty-seconds of the original sire is produced in group 14. By choosing parents from 6 and 8 the male line contains in group 12, twenty-seven thirty seconds of the blood of the original sire and five thirty-seconds of the blood of the original dam. If it is deemed advisable to vary the proportions of the blood of either side in any mating, groups 11 and 15 show that by selecting parents from 8 and 9, or 10 and 9, twenty-one thirty-seconds of the blood of either line and eleven thirty-seconds of the blood of the other may be obtained. Many other proportions may be worked out by combining different groups.

How, When and Where to Advertise.

The whole structure of the thorobred poultry business is built around advertising. If you have a good strain or variety of fowls it is your duty to let the world know about it. A sign painted on your poultry house or an ad placed in your local paper is not sufficient. Poultrymen would quickly starve to death if they depended upon this means of advertising.

Nor is it wise to win some prizes at the shows and expect to get a lot of free advertising because the poultry papers print the winnings. To expect to profit thus is to be of the consistency of a leach.

The poultry business is a billion dollar world wide business and you must get the vision and advertise to the whole world for you can ship stock or eggs most anywhere.

Where shall I advertise? The location of the publication has little to do with it. The character and size of its subscription list a great deal. You generally get just what you pay for and the publishers who charge more generally have larger circulations, not always. The make-up, style and general business policy of one paper may instill more confidence in its readers for its advertisers than another and thus two papers with equal circulation, one will pull far better than another. A safe rule to follow is to fish where the other fellows find fishing good. It may take you a long time to appreciate this and you may waste money on advertising in papers just because no other breed of your variety advertises there. You may win— once in awhile.

When shall I advertise? It is throwing money away to advertise a month or two, but after the second or third month you should be able to tell whether you have the right kind of bait in your ads. The successful advertiser changes his copy every month in the year and advertises every month in the year. Follow this rule and write your ads like you were writing a telegram—boil it down and re-write it a dozen times until you say just what you want to say. Then talk about the other fellow's needs and not your wants.

A good ad carefully worded and placed in the right publication is one of the best investments in the world. Advertising should be considered a privilege, not an evil necessity. The American poulterer can never repay the debt he owes to the progressive poultry publications in this country that have made the industry what it is. Read a few foreign poultry publications and you will appreciate what I mean.

Do not knock the poultry papers because they do not see fit to tell their readers about your fine birds or winnings when you do not advertise with them. If you show for the sport and have nothing to sell them you do not want publicity which will pester you with inquiries. If you have something to sell, then be honest and advertise and quit knocking the papers for not giving you a few dollar's worth of space gratis.

Brown Leghorn breeders as a class have been poor advertisers. Get in the game, the fishing is fine! The demand far exceeds the supply but the demand is in yonder states and provinces and you must advertise accordingly. A good rule to follow: Spend a half of what your feed costs each month in advertising. That rule will work wonders.

Keeping Fowls in Summer on City or Town Lot.

Fowls stand the close confinement of their houses and runs well in the winter time, but after a few weeks confinement in their small run in the spring time they cease to be active and alert. Their combs do not present the bright red appearance and they seem to pine and lose flesh, as a bird in a cage not accustomed to confinement.

There is more in keeping fowls in an intelligent manner and getting the highest efficiency out of them than merely keeping them in sanitary coops and runs and feeding them twice or three times a day. It is just as easy to keep the fowls the right way as it is the wrong way, no matter how few fowls you keep or how small the runs. The great mistake the town dweller with a small back lot makes is that he tries to keep too many on the lot he has. Numbers for the given space being equal, the experienced poultry raiser will make more off of his hens than the farmer who pays little attention to his fowls. It is because he gives them what they need and care and attention.

Fowls kept on the average city or town lot are an expense to the owner rather than making him anything when they are kept as the majority of fowls are kept in town. To make them pay for their feed and a little more they must be cared for properly. They must be kept in a sunny and dry house facing the south, with several windows of muslin or canvas to admit the fresh air. Their coops and runs must be kept clean and sweet. Dust must be provided for them to help free themselves of lice and mites. Hoppers should be provided in which are kept a constant supply of grit, charcoal, and oyster shells. Another hopper should be supplied with a good dry mash ration composed of two parts ground corn, one part bran, one part middlings, one part glutten feed, and one part beef scraps. With sprouting oats fed twice a week and scratch feed fed in six-inch litter of straw once or twice a day, the fowls will lay well during the winter and most of the summer. But to furnish them some diversion for their many days of confinement during the long summer when it is the hardest on them they should be provided with a run of fresh growing green food that will, as it were, take them back to the simple life.

It is an easy matter to do this if the sun shines on your back yard and you should not be guilty of keeping fowls where the sun will not shine. Poor, indeed, is the soil that will not grow an abundant crop of green forage food after being used

as a poultry run for some time. It is rich in the elements that make an abundance of plant life. It is a good policy to thin the flock in the early summer before they go to molting, as then they will not lay for several weeks anyway. After thinning out the flock somewhat you can easily divide the runs or parks into two parts. The accompanying photographs show how a small run fifteen by thirty feet was divided by stretching a piece of wire netting directly across, connecting two posts on either side. The run was then spaded up carefully and raked and sprinkled and reraked until the soil was pulverized thoroughly so the seed would have a good opportunity to grow. Much depends upon getting the soil in fine condition before planting. A mixture of lettuce, rape and millet seed was sown in this small patch, only a very small portion being rape and the majority being millet, as the rape takes up so much room

and the millet less. Rape seed is black, while millet seed is yellow, so I would suggest the proportion of one to ten. In three weeks' time the patch had made the growth shown in the photograph and the fowls were permitted to have a half hour each evening in it, care being taken that they did not trample it down, and when they were satisfied they were hustled back into the bare run.

In six weeks' time the patch had made the growth shown in the second picture, which looks more like a jungle picture

than a plot in a back yard. When it got this high the fowls could not trample it down and they were given their freedom so they would not disturb the root growth. Their enjoyment of this small run continued all summer until thrashing time came for the millet, when the fowls did this also, and how they did enjoy it.

In the first photo a grape vine may be seen growing in the wire netting which furnished some much needed shade. Also a few sun flowers are growing with the millet and rape to make more shade. They were planted earlier in the season in the runs and old buckets with the bottoms out placed over them to protect them from the fowls.

The question might be asked why I used the combination suggested? It is because millet makes the quickest and best growth and stands the late planting better than anything I know of except rape, and rape is such a succulent nutritious green food while lettuce grows quick and is tender and will be eaten first, giving the other plants a better chance when the fowls are first turned in.

The third photo shows another run and the provision made for shade on the south side with a row of sunflowers and a patch of sweet corn. Both poultry runs are situated on the same back lot, which is forty-nine feet wide and there is a plot of grass and flowers nineteen feet wide between the two parks so that there is no suggestion of the filthy and obnoxious poultry runs so often seen in the city or town. These parks remain sweet and fresh year after year and the fowls thrive under such intelligent treatment.

Poultry Appliances and Methods.

By ROY H. WAITE.

Economy Nests.

In October, 1917, the "Economy Nests," shown in figs. 1, 2, 3, and 4, were designed and six of our pens were equipped with them. These nests have been in use continuously since that time and have proven satisfactory in every way. They are equally serviceable for small or large breeds.

The principal advantage of these nests over most other designs is the economy of labor required to clean and keep them in a sanitary condition. In addition their construction requires a minimum of labor and materials, therefore they are also economical in this regard.

The wall of the poultry house serves as the back of the nest and as the whole section is hinged at the top, it can be swung out and propped up for cleaning, as shown in fig. 4, or the pin may be withdrawn from the hinges and the nests taken outside, if a thorough overhauling is thought necessary. The alighting boards are hinged to the front and may be raised

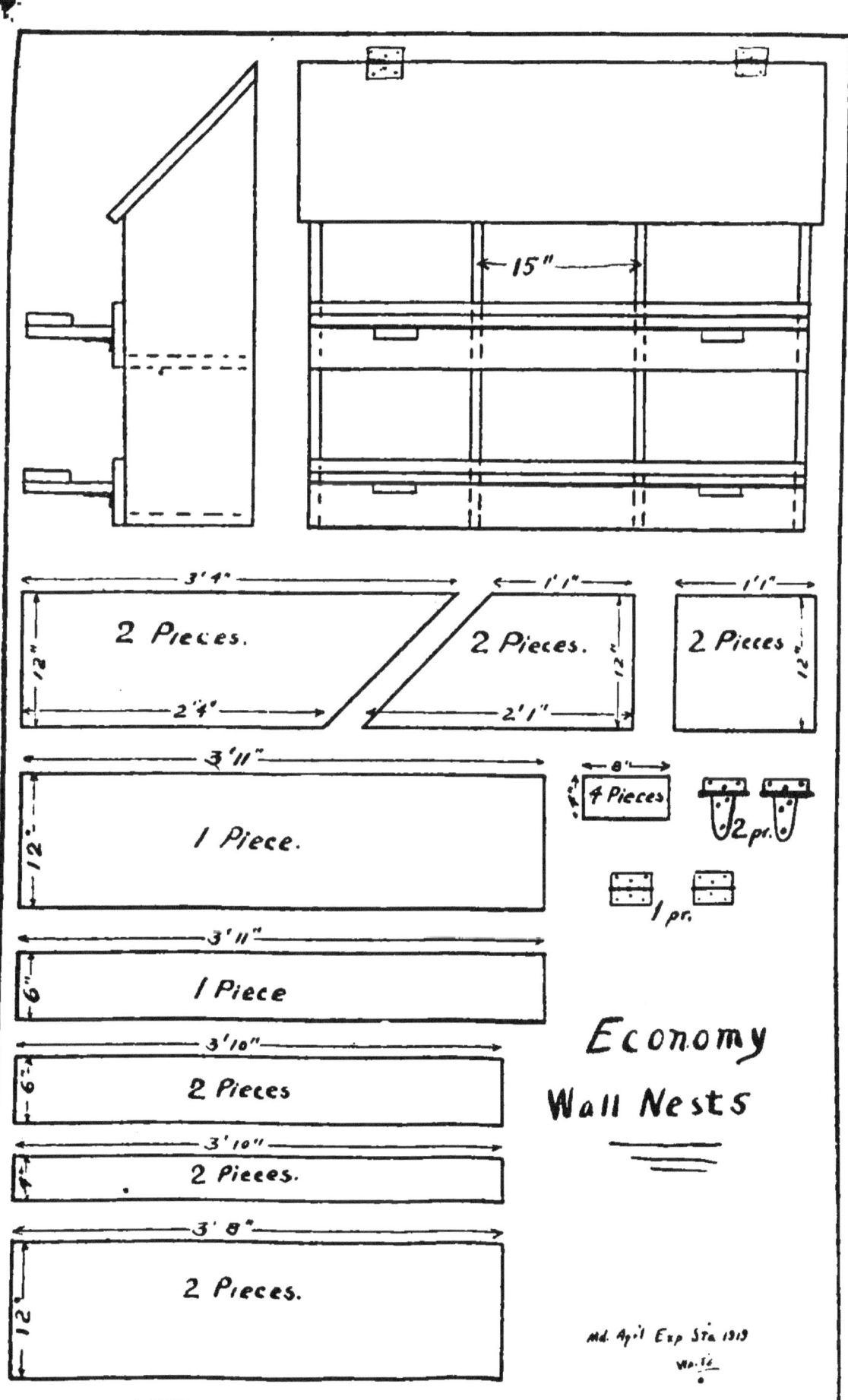

15"

3' 1"

2 Pieces.

1' 1"

2 Pieces.

1' 1"

2 Pieces.

12"

2' 4'

12

2' 1"

12

3' 11"

1 Piece.

12"

8"

4 Pieces

2 pr.

1 pr.

3' 11"

1 Piece

6"

3' 10"

2 Pieces

6"

3' 10"

2 Pieces.

3' 8"

2 Pieces.

12"

Economy

Wall Nests

Md. Agr'l Exp Sta 1919

No. 16

up and fastened to close the nests, as shown in fig. 3, or they may be left down so that the hens can enter (fig. 1). It is so often convenient to close nests at night, especially during moulting time, to keep the hens from roosting in them. Hens that do not moult till late fall, when the weather is cool, sometimes make considerable trouble for the poultrykeeper by persistently roosting in the nests. Pullets not accustomed to new quarters, often give trouble in this same manner.

Fig. 1—Economy Nest section open, ready for fowls to enter.

Each nest will serve from five to ten hens, therefore a section of six will accommodate a flock of from thirty to sixty birds. For smaller flocks sections of two or four nests each can be made. For larger flocks additional sections may be made if not thought too clumsy to handle.

The material required to construct a six-nest section is as follows:

Fig. 3—Economy Nest section closed.

Fig. 4—Economy Nest ready to clean.
Fig. 12—Simple Brood coop.

Fig. 5—Broody Coop made of electric weld lawn fencing.

2 boards—12 ft.x⅞ in.x 12 in.

2 board—12 ft.x⅞ in.x 6 in.

1 board—10 ft.x⅞ in. x 4 in.

1 pair loose butt hinges with screws.

2 pair strap T hinges with screws.

1 ℔. No. 8 finishing nails.

12 fence staples.

6 ft. number 9 wire.

"Broody Coop."

A slatted bottom "broody coop" has come to be recognized as almost an essential fixture for the poultry house. It is useful as a place where broody hens can be confined when it is desired to break them of setting and often comes in handy as a place for keeping surplus males during the breeding season or as a place in which to confine fowls for other purposes.

The broody coop shown in fig. 5 can be very easily and economically constructed. The sides and end are built of two-foot electric weld lawn fencing. A hole is cut into the front (1 fig. 6) made of the same fencing material is fastened in place by bending two of the line wires (fig. 6) of the door around the stay wire at the edge of the opening. The door swings on the

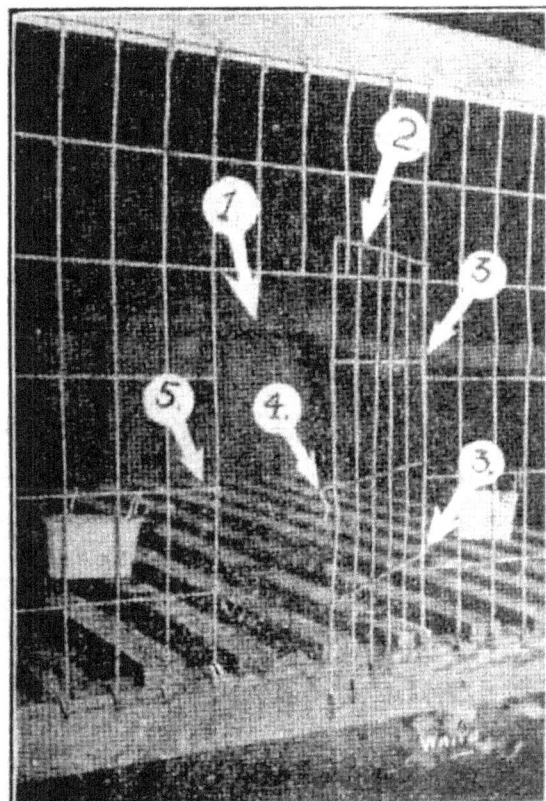

Fig. 6—Close up view of broody coop. (1) Opening. (2) Door. (3) Line wires. (4) Catch. (5) Line wire where catch hooks.

stay wire, the two bent wires acting as hinges. The catch is made by bending one of the line wires as shown in 4, fig. 6, and hooks over the line wire at 5, fig. 6.

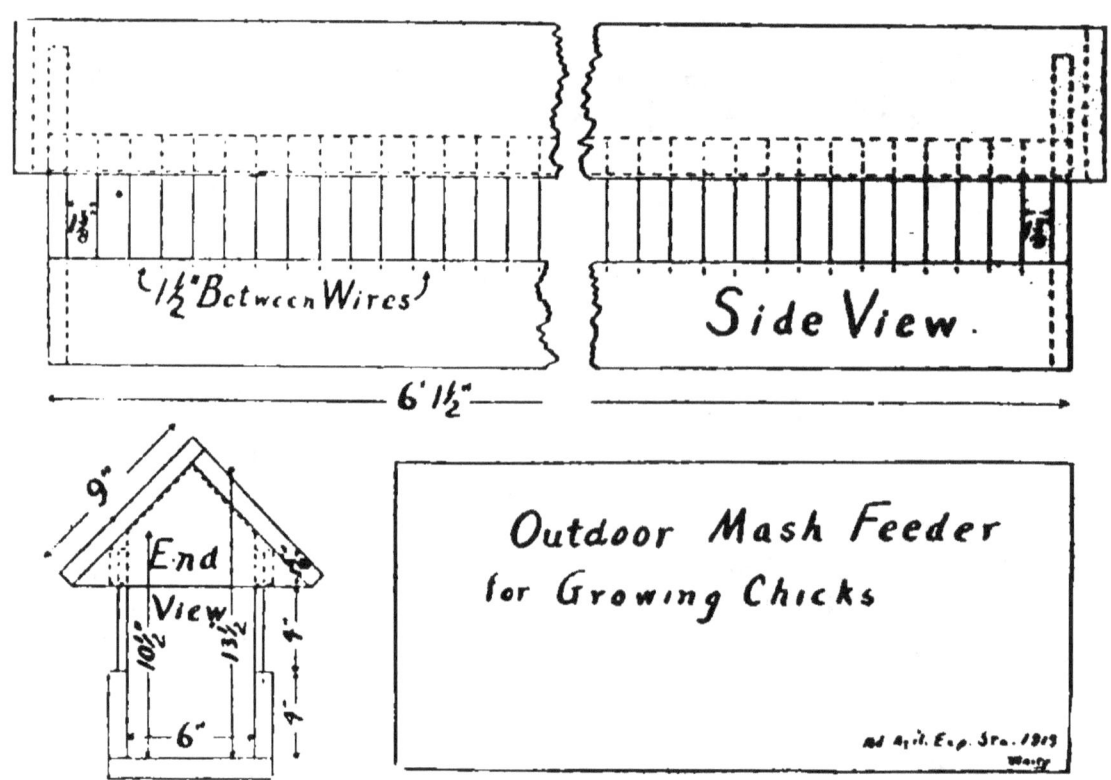

Fig. 7.

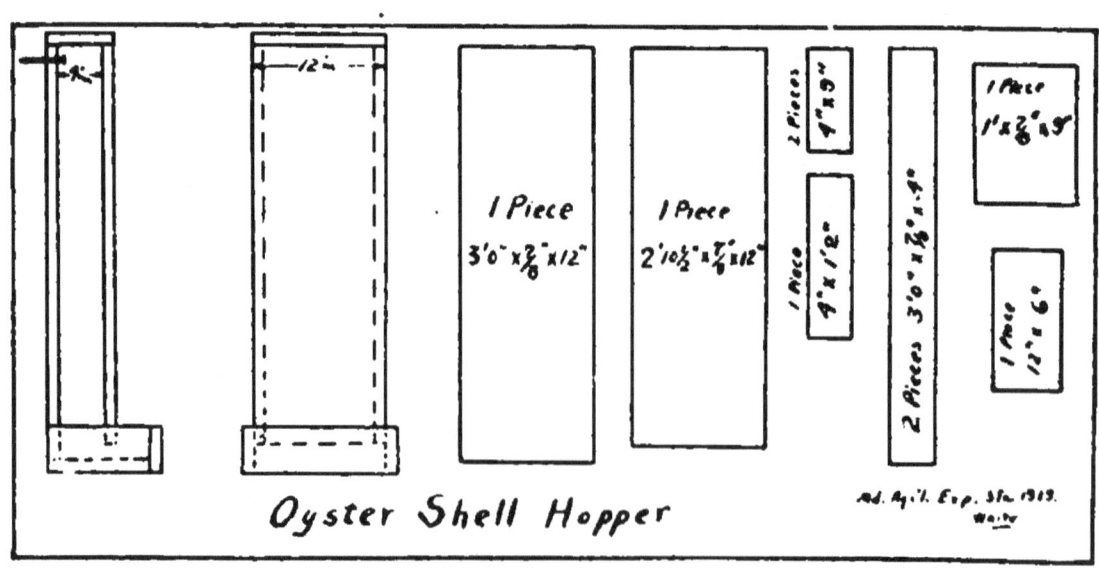

Fig. 8.

Out-door Feeder

The out-door feeder shown in fig. 7, has been used at this station during three seasons. This feeder differs from the usual slatted type in that the slats are replaced with short pieces of wire, making a neater construction, allowing more chickens to eat at the same time and letting more light enter so that the chickens can see the feed. The feeder shown in the drawing will serve from thirty to forty growing pullets up to the time they go into winter quarters. The feeder can,

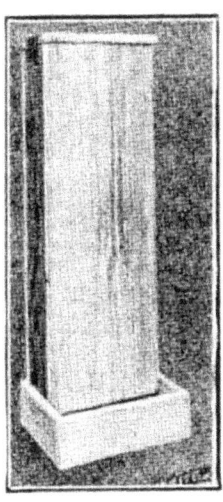

Fig. 9—Grit or shell hopper.

Fig. 10—Three compartment hopper.

however, be made in shorter lengths if the flocks are small.

There is practically no wasting of feed from feeders of this type, which is probably due to the fact that the light conditions make it unnecessary for the chickens to withdraw the head while eating

Shell and Grit Hopper.

The shell hopper shown in figs. 8 and 9 is of very simple construction and can be made by anyone who is at all handy with tools for all the pieces that go to make up this hopper are sawed with straight cuts. A decided advantage of this style over the ordinary shell hoppers is the greater capacity. Fig. 10 illustrates how the hopper can be constructed with three compartments.

Treatment for Scaly Legs.

Scaly legs are, as a rule, very troublesome, especially in flocks in which the brooding has been done with hens. The disease is not immediately dangerous, but fowls with scaly legs never do as well as those without. When it comes time to ship them to market fowls will not command as high a price per pound as clean legged specimens.

Fig. 11.

Kerosene oil has been found to be a cure for scaly legs but the method of applying it is apt to be somewhat tedious. A convenient method to cure scaly legs is to dip the legs in a tin can filled with kerosene oil. The can is filled and fastened to the wall of the house or other convenient place by driving a small nail through the end that is partly cut when the can is opened. Nailing prevents the can from being knocked over by the struggles of the bird and allows one person to do the work unassisted. It should be kept in the can as long as the disease is prevalent, so as to be convenient whenever there is an opportunity to dip

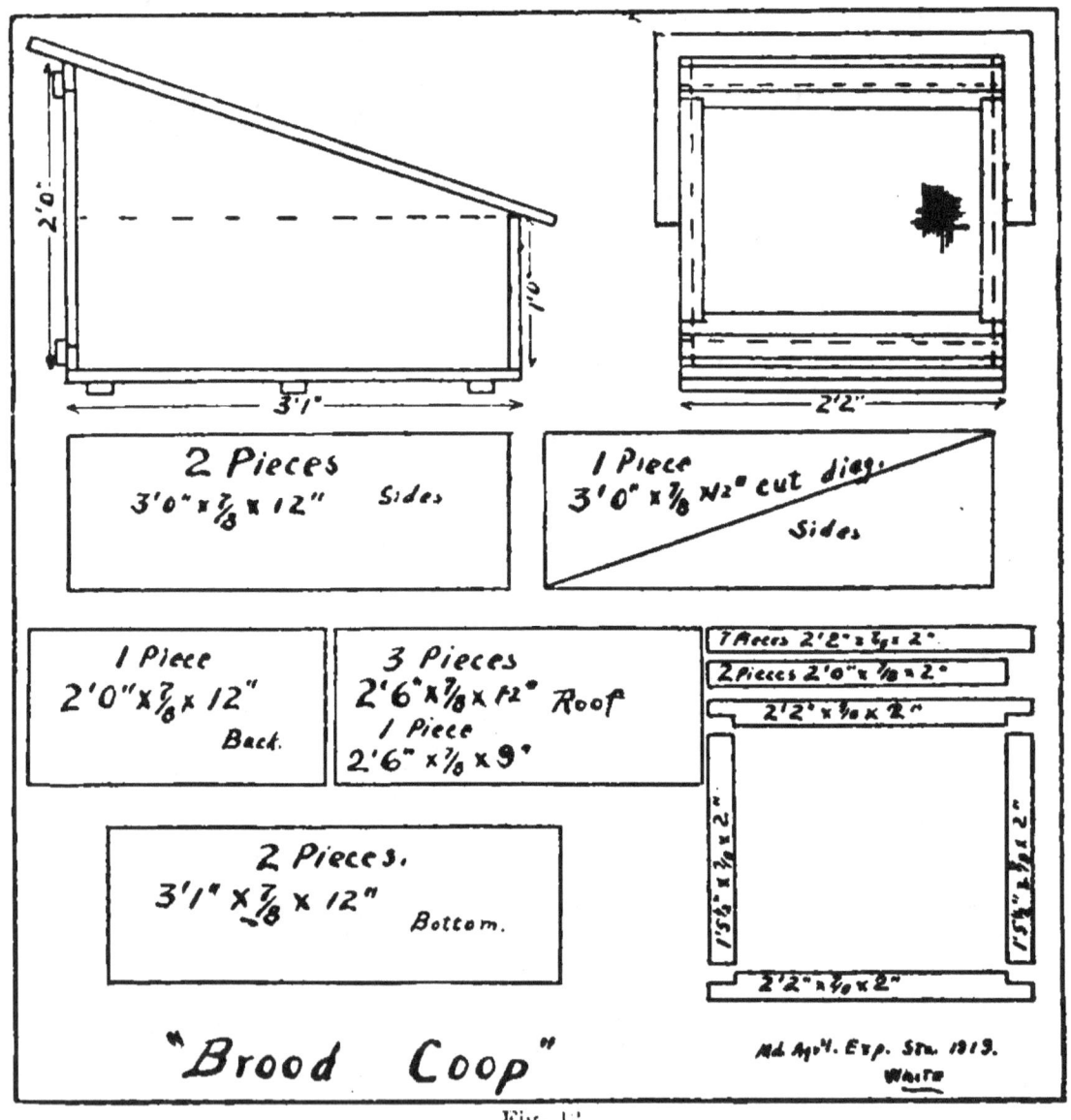

Fig. 12

the legs of the affected fowls, for more than one application will be required to effect a cure, especially if the disease is severe.

Simple Brood Coop.

This brood coop shown in figs. 11 and 12 is a very simple one to construct and makes an efficient "headquarters" for a hen and her brood of chicks. This coop can be used with or without a floor. When rats are troublesome or heavy rains prevalent the floor is a desirable feature. The door with its quarter-inch mesh wire cloth, covering fits closely to make the coop rat proof at night. During the day the door may be left slightly open, just enough to allow the chicks to run out and still confine the hen, or it can be opened wide when it is desired to let the hen have free range.

The material required to build one of these coops is as follows:

2 pieces 14 ft.x⅞ in. x 12 in.
2 pieces 12 ft. x ⅞ in. x 2 in.
1 piece roofing 30 in. x 4 feet.
1 piece wire cloth 2 ft. x 18 in.

Table of Contents

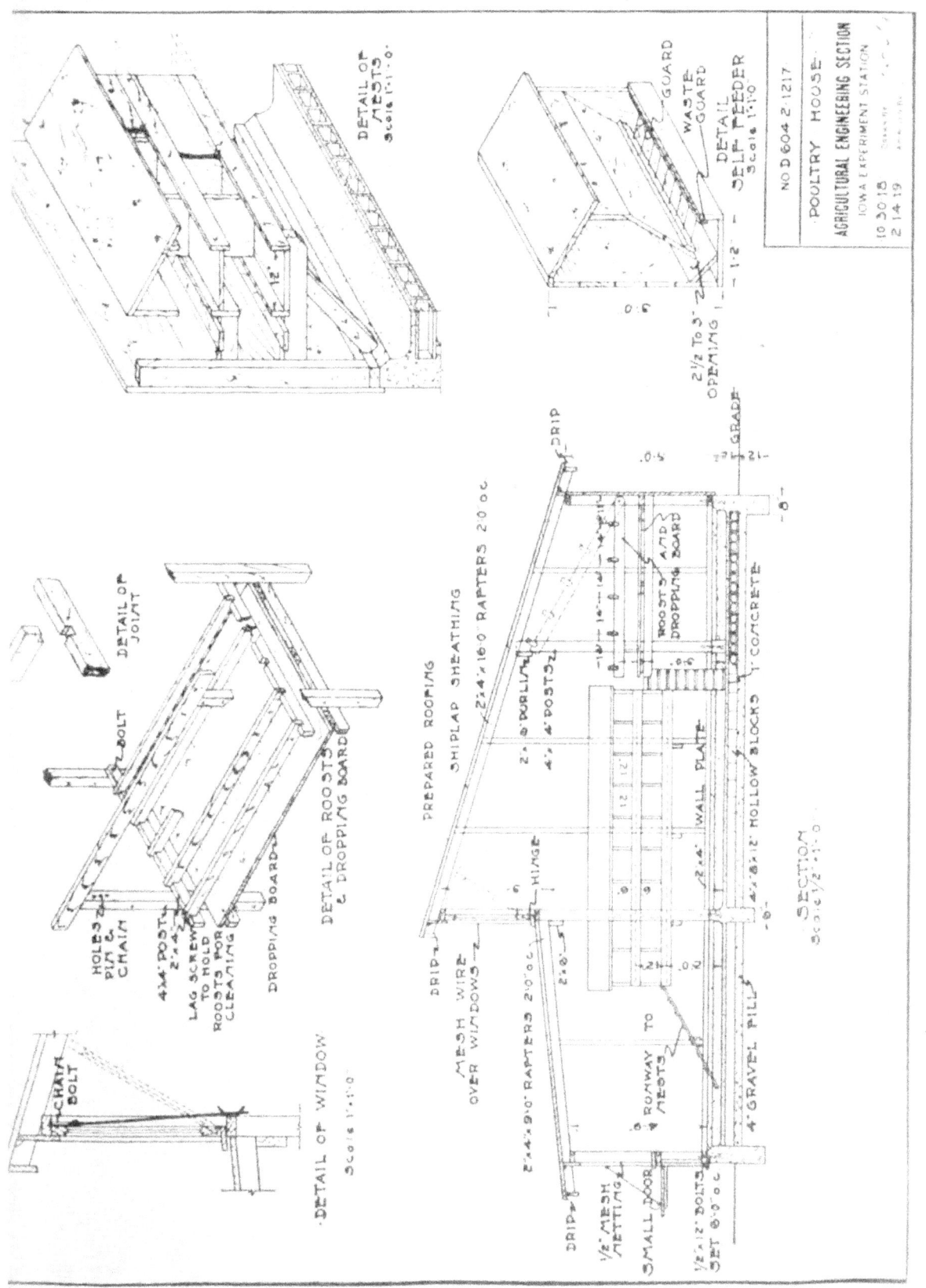

DETAIL OF NESTS
Scale 1"-1'-0"

DETAIL
SELF FEEDER
Scale 1"-1'-0"

GUARD
WASTE
GUARD

2½" TO 3"
OPENING

GRADE

NO D 604 2 1217

POULTRY HOUSE
AGRICULTURAL ENGINEERING SECTION
IOWA EXPERIMENT STATION
10 30 18
2 14 19

DETAIL OF
JOINT

BOLT

HOLES FOR
PIN &
CHAIN

4"x4" POST

2"x4"

LAG SCREW
TO HOLD
ROOSTS FOR
CLEANING

DROPPING BOARD

DETAIL OF ROOSTS
& DROPPING BOARD

CHAIN
BOLT

DETAIL OF WINDOW
Scale 1"-1'-0"

PREPARED ROOFING
SHIPLAP SHEATHING
2"x4"x16'0" RAPTERS 20"o.c.

2"x 6" PURLINS
4" POSTS

ROOSTS AND
DROPPING BOARD

1" CONCRETE

2"x4" WALL PLATE

4"x8"x12" HOLLOW BLOCKS

MESH WIRE
OVER WINDOWS

2"x4"x9'0" RAPTERS 2'0"o.c.

HINGE

RUNWAY TO
NESTS

½"x2" BOLTS
SET 6'0"o.c.

4" GRAVEL FILL

DRIP

½" MESH
NETTING

SMALL DOOR

SECTION
Scale ½" -1'-0"

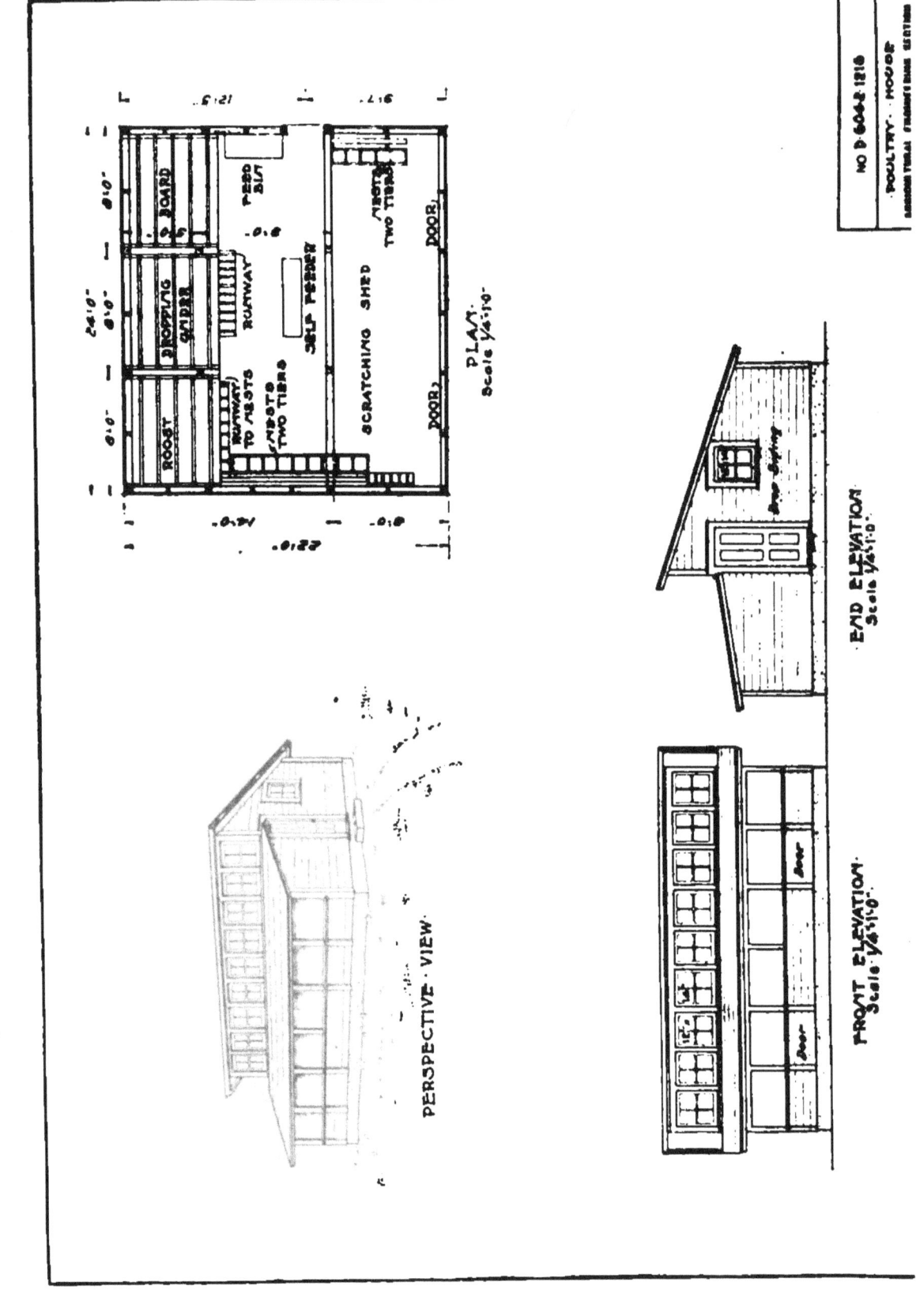

PLAN
Scale ¼"=1'0"

ROOST

DROPPING BOARD

NESTS TWO TIERS

RUNWAY

FEED BIN

SELF FEEDER

SCRATCHING SHED

NESTS TWO TIERS

DOOR

DOOR

PERSPECTIVE · VIEW·

END ELEVATION
Scale ¼"=1'0"

FRONT ELEVATION·
Scale ¼"=1'0"

Door

Door

NO D 604 F 1216
POULTRY · HOUSE